T3-BGM-282

0 3074 04570820 4

THE BIBLE &
THE BLACK MAN

BREAKING THE CHAINS OF PREJUDICE

CHANDLER PARK LIBRARY
12800 HARPER
DETROIT, MI 48213

OCT   2007

CP

CHANDLER PARK LIBRARY
12800 HARPER
DETROIT, MI 48213

OCT   2007

THE BIBLE & THE BLACK MAN

BREAKING THE CHAINS OF PREJUDICE

BY ROGER L. ROBERSON, JR.

TATE PUBLISHING & *Enterprises*

The Bible & the Black Man
Copyright © 2007 by Roger L. Roberson, Jr. All rights reserved.

This title is also available as a Tate Out Loud product. Visit www.tatepublishing.com for more information.

No part of this publication may be reproduced, stored in a retrieval system or transmitted in any way by any means, electronic, mechanical, photocopy, recording or otherwise without the prior permission of the author except as provided by USA copyright law.

All scripture quotations are taken from the *Holy Bible, King James Version,* Cambridge, 1611. Used by permission. All rights reserved.
Italics added by author. Some words have been modified from the sixteenth century English for easier comprehension.

The opinions expressed by the author are not necessarily those of Tate Publishing, LLC. This book is designed to provide accurate and authoritative information with regard to the subject matter covered. This information is given with the understanding that neither the author nor Tate Publishing, LLC is engaged in rendering legal, professional advice. Since the details of your situation are fact dependent, you should additionally seek the services of a competent professional.

Published by Tate Publishing & Enterprises, LLC
127 E. Trade Center Terrace | Mustang, Oklahoma 73064 USA
1.888.361.9473 | www.tatepublishing.com

Tate Publishing is committed to excellence in the publishing industry. The company reflects the philosophy established by the founders, based on Psalms 68:11,
"The Lord gave the word and great was the company of those who published it."

Book design copyright © 2007 by Tate Publishing, LLC. All rights reserved.
Cover design by Lynly Taylor
Interior design by Jacob Crissup

Published in the United States of America

ISBN: 978-1-6024724-5-7
07.05.31

We hold these truths to be self-evident, that all men are created equal, that they are endowed by their Creator with certain unalienable Rights, that among these are Life, Liberty and the pursuit of Happiness.

Preamble to the Declaration of Independence

DEDICATION

This book is dedicated to you, the reader. In the writing, it has been my goal to encourage you to be the "you" God intended, free from the chains of other's opinions or labels.

ACKNOWLEDGEMENTS

My thanks to "king" David Miller for his friendship, encouragement, and prayers for this work. David did what friends do, he believed with me.

Thanks also to my pastor, Dr. Billy Joe Daughtery,[1] for allowing the use of his photo, and to Doug Harrison for graciously permitting me to include his poem.

And a very special thanks to my best friend for the past forty-eight years, my wife, Euvon. As my first line editor, she patiently read, reread, corrected, and offered suggestions that helped to simplify many of the passages. A true help meet in every sense of the word. Thanks, Babe.

TABLE OF CONTENTS

FOREWORD

Dear Reader:

Do these two things before reading this wonderful book:

Buckle your safety harness for the ride of your life as you effort-lessly flow through one after another of these marvelous vignettes demonstrating the spiritual principles of wisdom, faith, and just say-ing "no" to ethnic hatred.

Comb your hair and brush your teeth because you are going to meet your Master in these Bible-laden pages.

Roger has drawn upon the Word of God, his own personal expe-riences, and extensive social research to produce a blockbuster of a book. His writing is effective in bringing the timeless verses of ancient Holy Writ into relevant treatment of the most urgent issues in our real-life world of conflict, prejudice, selfishness, and rebellion against our Maker. His pertinent illustrations have brightened my day and renewed my faith that a life of love is not only possible but is indeed attainable by those who will walk in holiness and consid-eration of one another.

This book is fair to all races and religions, though the author's bias in favor of the Matchless Son of God is obvious in every turn of the page. It is written as though the author were actually acquainted with the Great God of the Ages. This is so, despite the fact that it continuously relates stories that for someone far less psychologically mature would be personally humiliating. This gift of transparency lends an authenticity to the book that no amount of editing, ghost-writing, or book-doctoring could ever have achieved.

The author's many years of ministry, including the co-founding of Innocent Eyes International (with his wife Euvon), and teaching and working in the Sunday School Cell Ministry of Victory Christian Center, Tulsa, Oklahoma, have qualified him to write on these powerful topics of timely significance. He is currently working in the Sunday School as founding director of the Sunday School Ambassadors outreach program. He also works many hours behind the scenes preparing and mailing all of our new member mailings and many other projects. "Faithful" is written indelibly across the expanse of his lifetime of service for the Lord and for hurting humanity.

What is the purpose of this book? To call all of us to move swiftly away from our wicked prejudices and self-centered thoughtlessness and toward the desired state of having the love of God shed abroad from our hearts to all the inhabitants of the earth.

This book will make an important contribution to your understanding of these topics. In fact, it has implications for the entire world of Christendom, which has been occasionally accused of ethnic and other biases. At times the accusations have had some merit in actual fact, and at times the Church has been maligned. At any rate, the message of this book is that we must clean up our own house so that the hordes of lost pilgrims will come to know that there is a refuge of righteousness to which they may freely turn. The Church—as the extension of the heart of the Savior—must maintain its own purity in order to be available for satisfying the extensive love-hunger of a contentious world.

Roger Roberson's use of language is easily understandable and engaging. The active voice from which he speaks is obviously God-breathed and Spirit-inspired. Fasten your safety harness, turn the page, and let the adventure begin.

Cal Easterling, Ph.D.
Sunday School Superintendent
Victory Christian Center
Tulsa, Oklahoma

INTRODUCTION

The Bible records that, at the time, he was the only male in existence and she the only female. Yet Adam stood silently by as Eve ate of the forbidden fruit,[2] fully persuaded that she was about to die.[3]

Cain killed his only brother[4] simply because Abel was good.[5]

Lamech boasted to his wives that he had murdered two men because they had injured him in some way.[6]

Jacob exploited his brother's weakness in an effort to rob Esau of his inheritance.[7]

Rebekah conspired against her own husband in order to advance her favorite son.[8]

Joseph's brothers plotted his murder out of jealousy.[9]

And so it goes; from the very beginning until today—people hating, conspiring, robbing, lying, cheating, killing—hurting others. We think it worse today than it has ever been, but it is just as Solomon observed,

> "The thing that has been, it is that which shall be; and that which is done is that which shall be done: and there is no new thing under the sun. Is there any thing whereof it may be said, 'See, this is new?' It has been already of old time, which was before us."
>
> Ecclesiastes 1:9–10

and Jeremiah wrote,

> "The heart is deceitful above all things, and desperately wicked. Who can know it?"
>
> Jeremiah 17:9

Our own hearts testify to the truth of Jeremiah's allegation.

Every day we have opportunity to become irritated with another; frequently with persons we don't know, have never met, and most often, will never see again. Someone follows us too closely in traffic, accidentally jostles us in a crowd, or fails to say "Thank you," after we have opened a door for them.

More often however, the recipients of our irritation are those of our own family—wives, husbands, or children. It is estimated that in Los Angeles County alone, 200 children witness the murder of a parent each year.[10] Ever present within our hearts lies our true nature, poised to unleash against anyone that irritates or displeases.

Even Christians that boast of being "Spirit filled" often reflect more the personality of Satan than of God. Once while teaching a Sunday School class I made the comment, "If you want to know whether a person is truly Spirit-filled, slap them." One lady timidly raised her hand and asked, "Isn't there any other way?"

The point is that if someone is genuinely full of God's Spirit, they will not strike back at some small offense. When we are jostled, whatever is in us, whatever we are, will involuntarily spill out onto the offender.

Jesus said,

> "You have heard that it has been said you shall love your neighbor, and hate your enemy. But I say unto you, love your enemies. Bless them that curse you. Do good to them that hate you, and pray for them which despitefully use you, and persecute you."
>
> Matthew 5:43–44

During altar call on November 20, 2005, a man who had come requesting prayer struck Pastor Billy Joe Daugherty[11] in the face. Bleeding from a cut to his eye, Pastor Daugherty returned to the platform and continued the service, blood running down his face. He later visited the man to pray with him.[12]

Pastor's Black Eye

What jostles you, my friend? What offends? Many are offended at those of another culture, nationality, tradition, ethnic group, or color—even at those who hold different viewpoints or opinions.

For years, my wife and I taught a Sunday School class on basic Bible principles. The session ran eight weeks then would repeat. At some point during each session I would ask whether anyone had heard it taught that black skin was the consequence of God's curse upon Canaan.[13] No matter how small the class, always, at least one person would answer in the affirmative.

At one time in our history people of color were regarded as chattel.[14] In 1856, Dred Scott, a black slave, sued for his freedom. During the process he was declared the legal property of John F. A. Sanford of New York.[15] The decision, which was made in 1857, declared that no black—free or slave—could claim United States citizenship. It also stated that Congress could not prohibit slavery in the United

States territories. His case was appealed to the U. S. Supreme Court, which ruled he could not legally sue because blacks were not U.S. citizens. Shortly afterward, Scott was sold. His new owner gave him his freedom two months after the Supreme Court decision.

The years between 1865 and 1967 reflect one of America's darkest periods. It was during those years that more than 400 "Jim Crow" laws, constitutional amendments, and ordinances were passed legalizing segregation and discrimination against non-whites. Although the black populace was the primary target, Asians, Native Americans, and other minorities were included as well.[16]

Certain groups still advance those principles and attempt to use the Bible in support of their bigotry and to justify their claim of superiority. Among these "cream of the crop" are the Skinheads, the Neo-Nazis, the Ku Klux Klan, the Aryan Nation bunch, and even the widely acclaimed Planned Parenthood. (It would be interesting to know whether any of these individuals so vehemently opposed to dark skin, ever "lay out" in the sun to tan.)

In 1939, Margaret Sanger, founder of Planned Parenthood who had once stated, "*Colored people are like human weeds and are to be exterminated,*" launched the Negro Project. The Negro Project was an effort to dramatically reduce the number of blacks in America through the use of birth control and sterilizations.[17] Hear her in a letter to Dr. Clarence J. Gamble of the soap-manufacturing company Procter and Gamble, dated 10 December 1939.

"The [black] minister's work is also important and he should be trained, perhaps by the Federation[18] as to our ideals and the goal that we hope to reach. We do not want word to go out that we want to exterminate the Negro population, and the minister is the man who can straighten out that idea if it ever occurs to any of their more rebellious members."[19]

But what does the Bible teach? Do you know? As a matter-of-fact, just what *was* the sin so great that an entire people group should bear its judgement?

Well, that's the purpose of our journey here—to see clearly how God answers this damning, repressive, allegation. But don't accept blindly what is written here. Follow along in your own Bible as we look at a few revealing scriptures. We may even have a little fun along the way.

Yours in Christ,
Roger L. Roberson, Jr.

Everybody Is Somebody

He was not at all an impressive gentleman, just a simple, average, every day kinda guy. The leader of a small dance band, he played the clubs at night, slept and "hung out" during the days. Certainly he was no philosopher. But for a moment in time, he was right up there with Plato, Aristotle and the best of them. Our association was a brief one and after a few weeks we went our separate ways. I soon forgot his name, but I have never forgotten our first encounter.

It was during the early sixties and I was trying to launch a career as a songwriter. Doing everything I could think of to promote my songs, I often visited nightclubs in an effort to interest someone— *any*one—in my music.

One night I attended a nightclub in Cocoa, Florida. As I stepped into the dimly lit, smoke-filled room, an all black band was playing to a crowded dance floor, and they were good—*really* good. I immediately knew that I wanted to get them to a recording studio in Orlando for an audition.

When the set ended and the band broke for intermission, I went over to the one who seemed to be in charge and asked, "Are you the band leader?" When he answered yes, I said, "Well, my name is Bob.[20] I ain't nobody, but..."

Leaning back and feigning a look of amazement, he quipped in "old plantation" dialect, "Wha'chu *mean,* you ain't nobody? *Every*body *some*body! What is you, a *spook?*"

At the time we both had a good laugh. But over the years I found myself repeating the story many times to those who felt they weren't very important. Later, after becoming a Christian, I discovered "everybody is somebody" is one of the great principles of the Bible.

Think about it. Why did God so love the world, that He gave His only begotten Son, that *whosoever* believed in Him should not perish, but have everlasting life?[21]

And why is it that, the Lord is not slack concerning His promise, as some men count slackness; but is longsuffering to us-ward, *not willing* that *any* should perish, but that *all* should come to repentance?[22]

What would motivate One who is absolutely holy to sacrifice His only Son for an unholy bunch like you and me?[23] It's because everybody is somebody, my friend. *Everybody!*

CREATION, GOD'S COLORING BOOK

Color plays an important role in our lives every day. Many of our decisions are influenced by color—the clothes we wear, the car we drive, the decor of our homes...

Throughout the Bible, and most clearly in the letter to the Hebrews, we see that God patterned the world after His Heavenly Kingdom.[24] Even we represent His image and likeness.[25] Therefore, we can know that He has a passion for a kaleidoscope of colors, sizes, and shapes. It is evidenced everywhere we look—the sunrise and sunset, the rainbow, leaves of the trees, flowers...The whole earth explodes with His majesty, revealing His nature—His character.

> "The heavens declare the glory of God and the firmament shows His handiwork,"
>
> Palm 19:1

writes the Psalmist.[26] And the apostle Paul details more specifically.

> "The invisible things of Him from the creation of the world are clearly seen, being understood by the things that are made, even His eternal power and Godhead;[27] so that they are without excuse."
>
> Romans 1:20

One computer manufacturer claims its printer has the capability of reproducing more than sixteen million combinations of colors, and that from only three basic blends. If man can do that, how many more can the Master Designer produce?

Some colors we like better than others, but only in people do we dishonor and attempt to destroy color we don't care for. And so we understand that the issue is not about color of the skin but arrogance of the heart.

There are only two principals that determine one's eternal destination—our relationship with God and our relationship with others.[28] The apostle John writes,

> "If a man say, 'I love God,' and hates his brother, he is a liar. For he that loves not his brother whom he has seen, how can he love God whom he has not seen? And this commandment have we from Him, that he who loves God love his brother also."
>
> 1 John 4:20–21

From The World Book Encyclopedia[29] we read, "Light is a form of energy that behaves in some ways like waves. Light waves have a range of wavelengths. Different wavelengths of light appear to us as different colors. Light that contains all wavelengths in the same proportions, as sunlight, appears white. An object that reflects most of the light of all wavelengths in nearly equal amounts appears white. An object that absorbs most of the light of all wavelengths in nearly equal amounts appears black."

This can be seen and understood by directing a beam of light through a prism. The prism does not expose existing color, it simply reveals light *as* colors. Diamonds for example, when cut with many facets,[30] take on brilliance produced by the refracted light waves.

All colors then are of the same substance and from the same source—light. Colors do not exist *in* light, but appear by means *of* light. Again, from the World Book Encyclopedia: "Although we speak of seeing colors or objects, we do not actually see them. Instead, we see the light that objects reflect or give off."

In Genesis 1:1–3 we read,

> "In the beginning God created the heaven and the earth. And the

earth was without form, and void; and darkness was upon the face of the deep. And the Spirit of God moved upon the face of the waters. And God said, 'Let there be light,' and there was light."

As created, the earth was empty and dark, and therefore colorless. But as soon as light appeared, color appeared. We can better understand by thinking of lighting our homes. The potential to produce light exists as electricity. When applied to a suitable filament, light occurs in the room, and when light appears, color appears.

Color then is how an object *appears* to the eye based upon three scientifically established conditions: the length of light rays striking the object, its capacity to absorb or reflect those rays as determined by its composition, and the perception by the eye.

The key word for us is, *appears*. As light rays produce the appearance of colors in objects, so it is with people. This answers the question of where the black man came from—and the white, and the yellow, and the brown, and all shades in between.

Now that we understand that light waves produce colors, what produces light? Since science doesn't know, we turn to the Bible where we learn that the source of light is God.

> "This then is the message which we have heard of Him, and declare unto you," writes the apostle, John, "that God is light, and in Him is no darkness at all."
>
> 1 John 1:5

And again in Revelation 22:5,

> "And there shall be no night there; and they need no candle, neither light of the sun; for the Lord God gives them light: and they shall reign for ever and ever."

So then, since God *is* light, when He said "Let there be light," He was not creating light but imparting light to His creation. This helps us to see the difference between the *light*[31] in Genesis 1:3, and the created *lights*[32] in Genesis 1:14.

Not only is God Creator, He is artist, and He paints to delight the senses. But we must always be on guard because our senses are easily deceived. Paul informs us,

> "Now we see through a glass darkly[33] but then face to face. Now I know in part. But then shall I know even as also I am known."
>
> 1 Corinthians 13:12

Even Satan can make himself look good.

> "For such are false apostles, deceitful workers, transforming themselves into the apostles of Christ," writes Paul. "And no marvel, for Satan himself is transformed into an angel of light."[34]
>
> 2 Corinthians 11:13–14

Gossip, sarcasm, ridicule, bigotry—the illusion that we are more important than one of another color is demonic in nature and reveals an ignorance of truth.

Sowing Seeds of Hate

There are those who advance the position that the black man is the consequence of some sin. But if we're to indict the black man, we should know the crime of which he is accused. Some point to Canaan, others to Cain. Concerning Canaan, we need first to understand that it was not Canaan who sinned but his father, Ham.

> And Noah began to be an husbandman,[35] and he planted a vineyard. And he drank of the wine, and was drunken; and he was uncovered[36] within his tent.
>
> And Ham, the father of Canaan, saw the nakedness of his father, and told his two brethren without.[37] And Shem and Japheth took a garment, and laid it upon both their shoulders, and went backward, and covered the nakedness of their father; and their faces were backward, and they saw not[38] their father's nakedness.
>
> Genesis 9:20–23

"And Ham told..." The Hebrew word for told means, to report, manifest, to expose. Ham could easily have covered Noah himself and no one would ever have known. Instead he exposed his father to ridicule by telling his brothers, choosing to take "the low road" over the honorable.

> "Above all things," writes Peter, "have fervent charity[39] among yourselves: for charity shall cover the multitude of sins."
>
> 1 Peter 4:8.

"Hatred stirs up strifes, but love covers all sins."

Proverbs 10:12

"Honor your father and your mother, as the Lord your God has commanded you; that your days may be prolonged, and that it may go well with you, in the land which the Lord your God gives you."

Deuteronomy 5:16

and, finally,

"The nakedness[40] of your father, or the nakedness of your mother, shall you not uncover."[41]

Leviticus 18:7a

It would appear then that Ham had a character flaw—he lacked compassion. Therefore, it was Ham's character that would affect all his descendants, beginning with his son, Canaan. Look at it closely. It was Ham who committed the sin, yet Noah said "Cursed be Canaan," his son.

We can't see into Ham's heart to understand his motive, all we can know is what he did. He may have thought Noah's circumstance amusing—or disgusting. Or perhaps he just wasn't thinking. But whatever the reason, his conduct was disrespectful.

Those who would indict Cain claim that God marked him with blackness as punishment for the murder of his brother, Abel.[42] First, there is absolutely nothing in the Bible to associate blackness with Cain's mark. More importantly, the mark, whatever it was, was for Cain's *protection,* not his punishment.

And the Lord said unto him, "Therefore whosoever slays Cain, vengeance shall be taken on him sevenfold." And the Lord set a mark upon Cain, lest any finding him should kill him.

Genesis 4:15

Then there are those who teach that Jesus and Lucifer were brothers. The story goes that when Jesus was chosen over Lucifer to be Savior, Lucifer rebelled and a Great War was fought in Heaven.

Lucifer lost and was cast down to earth. Some of Adam and Eve's spirit children had fought against Satan halfheartedly and were sentenced to be born as mortals with black skin as a part of the lineage of Cain.[43]

These are seeds of hate, sown into the hearts of the ignorant and the arrogant—those who would be superior to other men.

SINS OF THE FATHER

And so was fabricated the lies that God marked Cain's, Ham's, or Adam's half-hearted warriors by darkening their skin and reducing them to servitude of their "uncolored" brothers.

The black man's accuser would point to Noah's statement,

> "Cursed be Canaan. A servant of servants shall he be unto his brethren...Blessed be the Lord God of Shem; and Canaan shall be his servant. God shall enlarge Japheth, and he shall dwell in the tents of Shem; and Canaan shall be his servant."
>
> Genesis 9:25–27

But this presents some serious problems. While Ham was the offender, he is not cited in the curse. On the other hand, Canaan is named in the curse but not in the offense. Noah did not say, "I curse Canaan," but, "Canaan *is* cursed." Therefore, the curse refers to the descendant, not the offender.

If it seems unfair that the son should suffer for the sins of his father, God agrees. In Deuteronomy 24:16 He said,

> "The fathers shall not be put to death for the children, neither shall the children be put to death for the fathers. Every man shall be put to death for his own sin."

Yet in Exodus 34 verses 6 and 7 we read,

> And the Lord passed by before him[44] and proclaimed, "The

Lord, The Lord God, merciful and gracious, longsuffering, and abundant in goodness and truth. Keeping mercy for thousands, forgiving iniquity and transgression and sin, and that will by no means clear the guilty; visiting the iniquity of the fathers upon the children, and upon the children's children, unto the third and to the fourth generation."

At first glance it may seem that God had a little trouble in making up His mind. But both statements are confirmed in our own society. For example, if a father commits a crime, even though only he is imprisoned, his entire family suffers.

The Biblical account of King Hezekiah gives us a clear example. In Isaiah chapter 38 and 2 Kings chapter 20, the writers record that Hezekiah, king of Judah, became very ill and God sent word for him to prepare to die. But Hezekiah begged for more time so God extended his life fifteen years.

Merodach-baladan, the king of Babylon, upon hearing of Hezekiah's illness and recovery, sent a delegation with letters and gifts of good will.[45] Hezekiah was so flattered by the attention he,

> ...showed them the house of his precious things, the silver, and the gold, and the spices, and the precious ointment, and all the house of his armor, and all that was found in his treasures. There was nothing in his house, nor in all his dominion, that Hezekiah showed them not.
>
> Isaiah 39:2

When Isaiah the prophet heard of the Babylonians visit, he asked the king what they had seen. Hezekiah answered, "I showed them everything."[46]

> Then said Isaiah to Hezekiah, "Hear the word of the Lord of hosts: 'Behold, the days come, that all that is in your house, and that which your fathers have laid up in store until this day, shall be carried to Babylon: nothing shall be left,' says the Lord.
>
> "'And of your sons that shall issue from you, which you shall beget, shall they take away; and they shall be eunuchs in the palace of the king of Babylon.'"

Then said Hezekiah to Isaiah, "Good is the word of the Lord which you have spoken." He said moreover, "For there shall be peace and truth in my days."

Isaiah 39:7–8

Hezekiah had become "puffed up" and committed a serious blunder.

But Hezekiah rendered not again according to the benefit done unto him; for his heart was lifted up. Therefore there was wrath upon him, and upon Judah and Jerusalem.

2 Chronicles 32:25

But he repented and was spared the consequences of his foolishness.

Notwithstanding Hezekiah humbled himself for the pride of his heart, both he and the inhabitants of Jerusalem, so that the wrath of the Lord came not upon them in the days of Hezekiah.

2 Chronicles 32:26

Nevertheless, although Hezekiah himself would not suffer, his sons and his nation would. When Nebuchadnezzar came to power in Babylon it happened just as God had said.[47]

Our children learn from us. Our qualities, good or bad, are passed on to them, and they have a propensity for following our example. We understand then that Genesis 9:25 is not a record of Noah placing a curse on Canaan, but the words of a wise father concerning the consequences of an immoral son. This might even be considered a warning for Ham to repent or his children, as in the case of Hezekiah, would be the casualties. Whether our decisions are wise or foolish, they always bear consequences. And so it was with Ham.

LIKE FATHER, LIKE SON

There's an old adage that says, "The fruit does not fall far from the tree," meaning, the son will tend to be like his father. The child does not always turn out as the parent, but the parent's influence upon his character is undeniable.

I once attended the trial of a father and son who together had violently assaulted a police officer. Both were arrogant and unrepentant.

In May of 2004, Wade Lay and his son, Christopher, entered the MidFirst bank in Tulsa, Oklahoma in a robbery attempt. When the bank guard tried to intervene, a gun battle ensued and the guard was killed. Tried for murder, both father *and son* were convicted. The son was sentenced to life in prison without the possibility of parole. The father was given the death penalty. At sentencing, the father made the following statement to the court: "I armed myself in resistance to tyranny. My son still thinks I'm right. The seeds have been planted. You may not want to accept that."[48]

Lamb and Lynx Gaede, beautiful thirteen-year-old[49] twins who made up the pop-music duo, *Prussian Blue,* were pictured in Newsweek magazine wearing T-shirts adorned with Adolph Hitler "smiley faces." A news camera crew followed the girls for several days as they sang and urged white people not to mix with other races. (Sample lyric: "Aryan man awake, How much more will you take, Turn that fear to hate, Aryan man awake.")[50] One can only imagine the influences that have, and are, shaping their young lives.

Then there are those average, hard working parents whose child has taken the wrong path. With broken hearts they lament, "Where did I go wrong? I did everything I could. I tried so hard to be a good parent."

There are many contributing factors, but one seems to stand out—neglect of the child's spiritual training. In Deuteronomy 6:6–7 and again in chapter 11:18–19, God said to the Israelites,

> "And these words, which I command you this day, shall be in your heart. And you shall teach them diligently unto your children, and shall talk of them when you sit in your house, and when you walk by the way, and when you lie down, and when you rise up."

First, God's Word must be in *our* hearts, then we must sow it into the hearts of our children. If we do these things, we are guaranteed success.

> "Train up[51] a child in the way he should go," wrote Solomon, "and when he is old, he will not depart from it."
>
> Proverbs 22:6

That isn't religion, my friend. If it works, it's just good common sense—and it does work.

One of the things my dad trained in me was to turn off the light whenever I left a room. Every time I left the light on he would say, "Son, I *told* you to turn off the light." He didn't tell me just once. He told me over and over and over, until I was tired of hearing it and he was tired of saying it.

But it worked. At the time of this writing I am seventy-two years old and I won't leave a room without first turning off the light, even if I'll be right back.

Whether we understand at the time or not, as a child matures into adulthood, seeds that shape his character are being sown into his life. And so it would appear that Canaan learned well from his father's example for, years later, because of their unrestrained depravity,[52] God commanded his descendants[53] to be driven from their land.[54]

Examining the Evidence

Having then laid the charge that black skin resulted from God's curse upon sin, evil men used the backs of the black man in an attempt to exercise supremacy. The difficulty with this is that the Bible never associates black skin with sin.

The color white, on the other hand, is a different matter. By blending fear and ignorance with the Levitical law, leprosy was viewed by the Jew as a sign of God's judgment. But leprosy turned one's skin white, not black.

> And the Lord said furthermore unto him, "Put now your hand into your bosom." And he put his hand into his bosom. And when he took it out, behold, his hand was leprous as snow.
>
> Exodus 4:6

> And the cloud departed from off the tabernacle; and, behold, Miriam became leprous, white as snow. And Aaron looked upon Miriam, and, behold, she was leprous.
>
> Numbers 12:10

> But he went in, and stood before his master. And Elisha said unto him, "Whence came you, Gehazi?"
>
> And he said, "Your servant went no where."
>
> And he said unto him, "Went not my heart with you, when the man turned again from his chariot to meet you? Is it a time to

> receive money, and to receive garments, and oliveyards, and vineyards, and sheep, and oxen, and menservants, and maidservants?
>
> "The leprosy therefore of Naaman shall cleave unto you and unto your seed for ever." And he went out from his presence a leper as white as snow.
>
> 2 Kings 5:25–27

Although the Bible equates sin as being black, it never equates black as being sin. As a matter-of-fact, the heroine of The Song of Solomon is a beautiful dark-skinned Shulamite maiden.[55]

Other evidence of God's acceptance of the black man is found in Acts 13:1, where we read,

> Now there were in the church that was at Antioch certain prophets and teachers; as Barnabas, and Simeon that was called Niger, and Lucius of Cyrene, and Manaen, which had been brought up with Herod the tetrarch, and Saul.

Here we are told that one of the notables of the early church was a man named Simeon, and that he was called Niger. Now the word niger means black. Therefore "Simeon called Niger" translates into, "Simeon, the black man."

And so we discover, as did Simon Peter, that God is no respecter of persons[56]—not male nor female, Jew nor Greek, white nor black.

Now, in *this* light, some black folk will want to reverse the complaint and apply the Bible against those of light colored skin. But the scriptures depict both colors in a positive as well as negative light. Therefore, whether black or white, none can either convict, or justify, on the basis of one's skin. The problem lies, not with the container, but the contents.

Jesus said,

> "A good man out of the good treasure of the heart brings forth good things. And an evil man out of the evil treasure brings forth evil things."
>
> Matthew 12:35

And again,

"Are you also yet without understanding? Do you not yet understand, that whatsoever enters in at the mouth goes into the belly, and is cast out into the draught? But those things which proceed out of the mouth come forth from the heart; and they defile the man.

"For out of the heart proceed evil thoughts, murders, adulteries, fornications, thefts, false witness, blasphemies. These are the things which defile a man: but to eat with unwashen hands defiles not a man."

Matthew 15:16–20

We may believe ourselves better than another, but God doesn't compare us to others—only to Himself. And that, my friend, leaves you and me woefully lacking, for *all* have sinned and come short of God's magnificence.[57]

Roses in a Tin Can

In season, roses bloom just outside our front door. Frequently I'll cut the prettiest, remove the thorns, and take them into the house for my wife. Now, we have flower vases, but I never can seem to find one. So, roses in hand, I'll look for anything that will hold water to use as a vase—a glass, a cup, an empty soup can—anything. The size, shape, material or color of the container isn't important. I just want something in which to put the roses. The treasure is the flower, not the container.

And so it is with God. He too has a treasure. In Colossians 1:25–27 Paul wrote,

> "Whereof I am made a minister according to the dispensation of God, which is given to me for you, to fulfil the word of God. Even the mystery which has been hid from ages and from generations, but now is made manifest to His saints to whom God would make known what is the riches of the glory of this mystery among the Gentiles, which is Christ in you, the hope of glory."

"Christ in you;"—the fulfillment of Jesus' promise to His disciples when He said to them,

> "And I will pray the Father, and He shall give you another Comforter, that He may abide with you for ever; even the Spirit of truth; whom the world cannot receive, because it sees Him not,

neither knows Him. But you know Him; for He dwells with you, and shall be in you."

John 14:16–17

God also is looking for "vases," as many as He can find. God is love,[58] but what good is love if you have no one with whom to share it? Jesus said to the Samaritan woman,

"But the hour comes, and now is, when the true worshippers shall worship the Father in spirit and in truth. For the Father seeks such to worship Him."

John 4:23

And neither is *He* interested so much in their outward appearance,[59] only that they hold the treasure. That was His plan from the beginning when He instructed Adam and Eve, and later Noah's family, to fill the earth with other "vases" just like themselves.[60]

Without a doubt the human body is a most remarkable creation. Nevertheless, in reality it is no more than an elaborate and complex piece of pottery.

"For we preach not ourselves," said Paul, "but Christ Jesus the Lord; and ourselves your servants for Jesus' sake. For God, who commanded the light to shine out of darkness, has shined in our hearts, to give the light of the knowledge of the glory of God in the face of Jesus Christ. But we have this treasure in earthen vessels, that the excellency of the power may be of God, and not of us."

2 Corinthians 4:5–7

From Mud to Man

When God formed Adam He did not give him His *Spirit*, only life.

> And the Lord God formed man of the dust[61] of the ground, and breathed into his nostrils the breath of life; and man became a living soul.[62]
>
> Genesis 2:7

The word used here for life is *chay*, meaning alive, and is not to be confused with *pneuma*, which implies *spirit*. The phrase, "*and man became*," reveals that when man was formed he was without life. Had not God breathed life into him he would have remained a mere statue, molded in God's likeness.[63] As one might fashion a vase from clay, so God formed man. Therefore we must acknowledge with Isaiah,

> "But now, O Lord, You are our father. We are the clay, and You our potter; and we all are the work of Your hand."
>
> Isaiah 64:8

> "O house of Israel, cannot I do with you as this potter?" said the Lord. "Behold, as the clay is in the potter's hand, so are you in My hand, O house of Israel."
>
> Jeremiah 18:6

And so we see Adam, a lifeless sculpture, transformed into a living "somebody."[64]

Every year small fortunes are spent on mud. We decorate our mud with attractive clothing and trinkets. We wash our mud, comb our mud, shave our mud, paint our mud, and splash our mud with sweet smelling waters to enhance its aroma.

Some have more mud than they want. Others feel they haven't enough mud, or the right kind, or the right color. While outwardly our mud may appear at peace and in control, inwardly our true riches often lie in confusion and disarray. Jesus expressed it this way:

> "Woe unto you, scribes and Pharisees, hypocrites! For you are like unto whited sepulchers,[65] which indeed appear beautiful outward, but are within full of dead men's bones, and of all uncleanness."
>
> Matthew 23:27

God's Word is clear. The Lord takes special note of each of us, even as we are being formed in the womb. Therefore, as with the Psalmist, we may say with complete confidence,

> "For You have possessed[66] my reins.[67] You have covered[68] me in my mother's womb. I will praise You, for I am fearfully and wonderfully made.[69] Marvelous are Your works, and that my soul knows right well.

> "My substance[70] was not hid from You when I was made[71] in secret[72] and curiously wrought[73] in the lowest parts[74] of the earth. Your eyes did see[75] my substance,[76] yet being unperfect;[77] and in your book all my members[78] were written,[79] which in continuance[80] were fashioned,[81] when as yet there was none of them.[82]

> "How precious also are Your thoughts unto me, O God! How great is the sum of them! If I should count them, they are more in number than the sand."
>
> Psalm 139:13–18a

We each of us are of great value, but no one more so than another.

> "For I say, through the grace given unto me, to every man that is among you," Paul cautions, "not to think of himself more highly than he ought to think; but to think soberly, according as God has dealt to every man the measure of faith."
>
> Romans 12:3

As remarkable as our physical bodies may be, we must remember that we are created beings. God made us, and He formed us of dust, as testified by David,

> "Know you[83] that the Lord, He is God. It is He that has made us, and not we ourselves. We are His people, and the sheep of His pasture."
>
> Psalm 100:3

> "For He knows our frame; He remembers that we are dust."
>
> Psalm 103:14

by Job, the patriarch,

> "All flesh shall perish together, and man shall turn again unto dust."
>
> Job 34:15

and by God Himself.

> "In the sweat of your face shall you eat bread, till you return unto the ground; for out of it were you taken: for dust[84] you are, and unto dust shall you return."
>
> Genesis 3:19

In spite of our best efforts, my friend, in the end our mud dries, wrinkles, shrivels, crumbles, and returns to the earth. One day the "beautiful" and the "homely" will all look the same.

> One dies in his full strength, being wholly at ease and quiet. His

breasts are full of milk, and his bones are moistened with marrow. And another dies in the bitterness of his soul, and never eats with pleasure. They shall lie down alike in the dust, and the worms shall cover them.

Job 21:23–26

This is one truth of the Bible that atheists, evolutionists, and other nay-sayers can not dispute. Not only does Science bear this out, we may see for ourselves. All we need do is to look inside an old grave. Where once lay an "us," now there is only dirt and perhaps a few bones. Why then do we spend so much of our time and resources on the temporary us and so little on the eternal us?

Obsession with our mud breeds self-worship and a spirit of arrogance, while discontentment breeds discouragement, depression—a feeling of inferiority.

Though our physical *us* is wonderfully made, our spiritual us needs some fixing up. God has not honored us by referring to us as "sheep." Sheep are feeble, my friend. They are naturally smelly, essentially dirty and, well—not very bright. They have neither ambition nor direction. Without a shepherd they would live their entire lives wandering aimlessly about. That's how God views us.

"All we like sheep have gone astray," writes Isaiah. "We have turned every one to his own way."

Isaiah 53:6a

Dr. J. Vernon McGee, a renowned minister, told of a time when he and another minister spoke at an event. Afterwards, a number of people approached his friend commenting on his wonderful message. Dr. McGee said he heard his friend mutter under his breath, "Lord, don't let me get puffed up." But one man was not impressed and said so in no uncertain terms. Dr. McGee said he then heard his friend mutter, "Lord, please don't let me get puffed down."

A good trick if you can pull it off. Personally, I sometimes have a little trouble with the balance.

Oh, No! It's Me

It began as soon as I walked through the door. Customers sniffed the air, wrinkled their noses, and screwed up their faces.

"What's that *smell?*"

"Do *you* smell that?"

"Smells like *skunk!*"

The back door to the establishment was open so one of the ladies closed it, thinking to shut out the odor. Not a helpful move since the offence was not from the outside. I didn't have to wait for service. I was escorted straight to a chair. Becoming a little suspicious I asked the barber, "Did you guys just begin to notice the smell when I came in?"

"Yes. But that's all right. It's not so bad."

Oh no, I thought. *It's me.* I searched my mind for what it could be. "We just had a new windshield installed on our car yesterday," I told the lady. "Maybe it was something the mechanics used in sealing it and the odor got onto my clothes."

"Could be," she agreed. Yeah, that's a possibility.

Nevertheless, after finishing with my hair she walked me straight to her car, insisting I accept a can of her favorite air freshener, promising it would do wonders for the smell in the car—(she meant *me*). My wife and I had been noticing a faint (in my defense I emphasize the word, faint) unpleasant odor the last few days but assumed our little poodle was having some "doggie problems." Boy, were we wrong.

"Smells like skunk," said the vet. Evidently a skunk had ventured into our back yard and taken a shot at our little dog—not a direct hit, but close enough. Since I had continued playing with him my clothes picked up the scent. Thus, growing accustomed to the smell, I became an unwitting carrier, sharing brother skunk's unique greeting with everyone with whom I came in contact.

So it is with mankind. Our dilemma lies in the fact that we are descendants of Adam and Eve—sinners, both. Consequently, we are sinners by birth and are accustomed to the smell. Sin, my friend, is ours by inheritance. Like it or not, we all enter the world physically as babies, and spiritually as sinners.

> "Behold," writes the Psalmist. "I was shaped in iniquity, and in sin did my mother conceive me."
>
> Psalm 51:5

We may protest, "But little babies haven't done anything wrong." That's true. But as with all humanity, even little babies fall short of being as glorious as God.

From the very beginning life is all about *me*. Feed *me!* Change *me!* Hold *me!* That's what the crying is all about. No, man does not have to learn self-will. He is born with that. What he must learn is discipline in the way of obedience. Remember, we are not sinners because we sin. We sin because we are sinners.

Not everyone has sinned the same as did Adam.[85] As a matter of fact, the world is full of wonderful and caring people. In the letter to the Roman Christians, Paul writes,

> "Tribulation and anguish, upon every soul of man that does evil, of the Jew first, and also of the Gentile. But glory, honor, and peace, to every man that works good, to the Jew first, and also to the Gentile.
>
> "For there is no respect of persons with God. For as many as have sinned without law shall also perish without law. And as many as have sinned in the law shall be judged by the law. For not the hearers of the law are just before God, but the doers of the law shall be justified.
>
> "For when the Gentiles, which have not the law, do by nature the things contained in the law, these, having not the law, are a law unto themselves, which show the work of the law written in their hearts, their conscience also bearing witness, and their thoughts the meanwhile accusing or else excusing one another."
>
> Romans 2:9–15

What Paul is saying is that, being a sinner does not automatically make one *evil*. Jesus said,

> "A good man out of the good treasure of his heart brings forth that which is good; and an evil man out of the evil treasure of his heart brings forth that which is evil. For of the abundance of the heart his mouth speaks."
>
> Luke 7:45

The Bible draws a clear distinction between good and evil persons. Abel was the very first the Bible records as good.[86] Following were Seth, Enoch, Noah, Abraham, Job, David, Ruth and others. But not only they, all through the ages multiple millions of individuals have led lives of kindness and self-sacrifice. Even so, none have ever been able to measure up to the perfection of a Holy God, for all have fallen short of His glory.[87]

No Exceptions

All means *all*, my friend. All means *me*—it means *you*. White, black, yellow, red, brown, male, female, short, tall, fat, skinny—we *all* are equal in the eyes of God—from the President, to the Supreme Court Justices, to our nation's homeless and destitute. He does not favor according to one's color, heritage, or gender—not even whether Jew or Gentile. Speaking from a revelation from God, Paul taught,

> "There is neither Jew nor Greek, there is neither bond nor free, there is neither male nor female: for you are all one[88] in Christ Jesus."
>
> Galatians 3:28

And to the Colossians he wrote,

> "Lie not one to another, seeing that you have put off the old man with his deeds; And have put on the new man, which is renewed in knowledge after the image of Him that created him: Where there is neither Greek nor Jew, circumcision nor uncircumcision, Barbarian, Scythian, bond nor free: but Christ is all, and in all."[89]
>
> Colossians 3:9–11

Bigotry is discrimination, but bigotry does not discriminate. It does not select by color, only hearts. The black man rightfully accuses the white man of enslaving his people while conveniently evading the fact that his ancestors are equally as guilty.[90] Slavery could not have flourished as it did without the active and enthusiastic participation of the black man. Powerful African tribes descended upon the weaker, sometimes selling entire villages to the white slave trader or to other black tribes—women and children as well as the men.[91]

> "Africans had practiced slavery since ancient times. In most cases, the slaves had been captured in warfare and sold to Arab traders of northern Africa. The Europeans obtained slaves from black Africans who continued to sell their war captives or trade them for rum, cloth, and other items, especially guns. The Africans needed the guns for use in their constant warfare with neighboring peoples."[92]

Khalid Muhammad, aide to Louis Farrakhan,[93] proclaimed to students on college campuses, "We will kill everything white...We kill the women, we kill the children, we kill the babies...we kill the faggot, we kill the lesbian, we kill them all."[94]

Chinese slaughter Chinese. Koreans exterminate Koreans. Native Americans justifiably accuse the Europeans of stealing their lands and decimating their people. But hostilities existed between their tribes long before the Europeans descended upon them. Today we see destruction the world over. Nations are ripped asunder by civil disobedience, rebellion and conflict.

Joseph Stalin of the late USSR massacred an estimated forty to sixty million of his own peoples. Adolph Hitler of Germany, Benito Mussolini of Italy, Idi Amin of Uganda, Mao Tse-tung of China, Pol Pot of Cambodia, Kim Jong Il of North Korea, Saddam Hussein of Iraq—mankind against mankind—whites against whites—blacks against blacks—religions against religions—wars and rumors of wars.[95]

And while we "civilized" condemn these men for the horrors they inflict upon humanity, we conveniently close our eyes to those medical mercenaries who wage their own brand of genocide against the helpless—the unborn.

Physical and sexual abuse, homosexuality, incest, murder, pedophilia, rape, human trafficking, white slavery—man's passion for the bestial is infinite and indiscriminate. Color is only one of many pretexts man invents in an attempt to justify his depravity.

Adam's rebellion was not just a personal failure. It unleashed an eruption of savagery, hate and intolerance into all of creation.[96] Even as you read, the unscrupulous execute genocide upon their own people as well as others. News reports it—history records it—our own hearts affirm it.

Oh no, my friend. Arrogance is not a disease confined to one people. Finding opportunity in the heart of Adam it instantly infected all mankind, beginning with Eve, and progressing to their very first son.

> And Cain talked[97] with Abel his brother. And it came to pass, when they were in the field, that Cain rose up against Abel his brother, and slew him.
>
> Genesis 4:8

But we cannot charge everyone with being evil hearted. Not everyone has defied God as did Adam.[98] While he consciously rebelled, Eve was deceived.[99] So it is with the vast majority of all peoples. Most are essentially honest and hard working, wanting no more than to live a peaceful, productive life.

Even of the Pharisees there were those who befriended Jesus.[100] Some became His disciple.[101] There were also Roman soldiers who loved God and treated the Jew kindly.[102] And there are those many individuals today who do what is right simply because it is in their heart.[103]

However we all have made decisions and done things that grieved God's heart.[104] That too is sin. Since then we all have sinned, and the wages of sin is death, we all are under the sentence of death.

> Wherefore, as by one man sin entered into the world, and death by sin; and so death passed upon all men, for that all have sinned.
>
> Romans 5:12

THE PROWLING LION

Many who profess to be Christian and to love God, have difficulty with people relationships. Yet God commands us to love others as well as Himself.[105] Sometimes that isn't easy to do. Even children have their people challenges.

One little girl wrote, "Dear God, I bet it's very hard for you to love all of everybody in the whole world. There are only four people in our family and I can never do it." Nan.

Others wrote:

"Dear God, if we come back as something, please don't let me be Jennifer Horton—because I hate her." Denise

"Dear God, Did you really mean 'Do Unto Others As They Do Unto You,' because if you did then I'm going to fix my brother." Darla.

"Dear God, Please send Dennis Clark to a different camp this year." Peter.

Then there are those who think people are OK, but pets are preferred.

"Dear God, Thank you for the baby brother but what I asked for was a puppy. I never asked for anything before. You can look it up." Joyce.

Finally, one little boy with the wisdom of Solomon, solved the whole people issue.

"Dear God, Maybe Cain and Abel would not kill each other

so much if they had their own rooms. It works with my brother."
Larry.[106]

Soon after becoming a Christian, I ushered for a performance of
Jesus Christ, Super Star. The following day a friend visited our home.
During our conversation she asked what I thought of the way in
which Jesus had been portrayed. As we talked, she began to criticize
the church.

In an attempt to defuse the tenseness of the moment, I replied
laughingly, "Hey! Don't talk about my church." At that, her expres-
sion changed, becoming uncharacteristically brusque—menac-
ing. Leaning forward in her chair she challenged, "Oh! So it's *your*
church!"

I tried to change the subject but she persisted. My wife and I were
stunned. This was one of our dearest, sweetest, friends. Her behavior was completely out of character. Not knowing what else to do, I
excused myself and went for a drive.

When I returned, my wife said that our friend had gone home and
called back, devastated and in tears. Apologizing profusely, she said
she did not know what had come over her. This wonderful lady was
not a Christian at the time. Neither was she "demon possessed." But
for that moment, Satan had used her just as he had the serpent in
the garden and the Roman soldiers who crucified Jesus.[107]

God has an enemy my friend. His name is Lucifer.[108] He is the
devil,[109] the accuser of mankind. Like the thief that he is, he comes
only to steal, to kill and to destroy God's seed.[110]

> "The sower sows the word," Jesus explained. "And these are they
> by the way side, where the word is sown. But when they have
> heard, Satan comes immediately, and takes away the word that
> was sown in their hearts."
>
> Mark 4:14–15

Satan is quick to cast doubt upon God's Word because it increases
our confidence *in* God,[111] and what we believe governs what we do.[112]
His method is singular and resolved. The same ruse he used on
Adam and Eve[113] and attempted with Jesus,[114] he will try on us. He
appeals always to our desires and our pride.[115]

Appearing as a messenger of light,[116] he strokes our ego with visions of grandeur. He promotes self-esteem, filling us with illusions of being more knowing, more important—better than someone else. He was at work in the beginning and is at work still—wooing, flattering, and misleading the unwary. Appealing to our passion for pleasure, he lures us into his ungodly alliance.

But God warns that the pleasures of sin are temporary at best,[117] ending always in disappointment within and strife without. We must not take Satan lightly. He is a formidable adversary.[118] Alone we are helpless against his assaults. But God has not left us alone. From the beginning, He promised to send One who is able.

In Genesis 3:15, God spoke to Satan, the spirit behind the serpent, predicting his future destruction.

"And I will put enmity[119] between you[120] and the woman, and between your seed[121] and her Seed.[122] It[123] shall bruise your head, and you shall bruise His heel."

Satan is the master of deception.[124] He is the destroyer. His allies are not only demons[125] but people also—those who are willing accomplices,[126] and those who are seduced.

And Adam was not deceived, but the woman being deceived was in the transgression.

1 Timothy 2:14

Even you and I have been his unsuspecting pawns at one time or another. And unless we are aware of his craftiness we will, without a doubt, serve him again. We must always be on our guard, for Satan will attempt to use us in destroying ourselves as well as others.

The most damning evidence of his activity today is the millions of aborted babies—blood sacrifices to the god of self. Victims of the holocaust of the Jew during World War II have been estimated at six million. The holocaust of the unborn has exceeded fifty million in the United States alone,[127] and increases hourly. Many who decry the Nazi concentration camps hypocritically support the systematic destruction of little ones as they lie helpless in their mother's womb—no strength to fight, no way to run, no place to hide.

But abortion is neither new nor unique to the world. At the time of this writing, abortion is customarily associated with the unborn. But its basic definition means simply the premature ending of a life. Satan was in the abortion business from the beginning, Abel being his first victim.

Moreover, the seed of destruction that originated in his evil heart, he has sown into ours. No, what man chooses to call the termination of an unwanted pregnancy, God calls the murder of a wanted human being. It is God's will and purpose that *every* man, woman and child, born or newly conceived, come to enjoy a personal, intimate relationship with Him in His kingdom throughout all eternity.

As Jesus said to the twelve, He says also to every believer.

> "Let not your heart be troubled. You believe in God, believe also in Me. In My Father's house are many mansions: if it were not so, I would have told you. I go to prepare a place for you. And if I go and prepare a place for you, I will come again, and receive you unto Myself; that where I am, there you may be also."
>
> John 14:1–3

THE TIGER WITHIN

Siegfried Fischbacher and Roy Uwe Ludwig Horn were Las Vegas headliners who made large white tigers appear and disappear in their act. On October 3, 2003, Roy was mauled by one of the tigers during a performance. Bitten on the neck by a seven-year-old male tiger, Roy was critically injured and sustained severe blood loss. For a time, it was doubtful that he would survive. But in due time Roy did recover.

A number of explanations were put forth as to what actually happened, most in defense of the tiger. Some say that Horn had fallen and that the tiger, thinking him injured, was attempting to drag him to safety. But regardless of the intent, the consequences were severe and almost fatal.

Roy was well able to train and control the tiger's behavior up to a point, but he could not master his heart. At a very crucial moment the tiger had simply behaved like a tiger. And so it is with sin. We may think we have our passions under control. But just as Roy Horn's tiger turned on him, in due time, they will turn to destroy us.

Roy's plea that the tiger not be destroyed is reminiscent of the demon possessed man of Gadara, who did not want to lose his personal demons.[128] It also pictures those who want to hold on to habits and lifestyles that are destroying them.

Jesus explained:

"For this people's heart is waxed gross, and their ears are dull of hearing, and their eyes they have closed; lest at any time they should see with their eyes, and hear with their ears, and should understand with their heart, and should be converted, and I should heal them."

Matthew 13:15

"And this is the condemnation, that light is come into the world, and men loved darkness rather than light, because their deeds were evil."

John 3:19

MARSHA'S OLD MAN

John was an "on fire for Jesus" Christian who married an unbeliever named Marsha. Soon after their wedding, John began praying for Marsha's salvation, which irritated Marsha no end. When John prayed, Marsha would scream at him to stop. When he persisted, she would explode with anger—sometimes even to the point of throwing things at him.

So John wisely began waiting until night when Marsha was asleep. Then he would kneel at the foot of their bed and pray. Frequently, Marsha would wake and kick furiously at his head and face to get him to shut up. She just didn't want to get saved.

Nevertheless, John was determined and kept praying for Marsha's soul. But before praying, he began taking a firm grip of her ankles to control the kicking. It continued like that for some months. John kept praying. Marsha kept resisting.[129]

Then one Sunday the preacher spoke on man's fallen nature. When the altar call was given, the invitation was for anyone having trouble with "the old man." By this time Marsha had had about all she could take of John and his constant praying.

That's me! she thought. *Boy! Am I ever having trouble with the old man!* So, thinking the pastor would help her in straightening out John, she went forward. That morning, Marsha settled accounts with her "old man."[130] Marsha got saved. When we met John and Marsha they were travelling together as evangelists, ministering hope and healing to others.

At the center of sin is "the big I"—the "number one"—the "old man." Absorbed with self, we often are oblivious to how offensive our natural man is to our Creator and, frequently, to others. Oh, there's no question but that God loves us.[131] And I love our little dog. It was not his fault the skunk sprayed him. He was just an innocent bystander. But that didn't keep him from smelling.

So it was with Marsha, and so it is with us all. Conceived in sin,[132] we all need a new nature. We all need a new beginning.

No Place to Hide

Since God Himself tells us the heart is deceitful above all things, and desperately wicked,[133] some would attempt to defend their misbehavior by indicting God. "It's not my fault. That's the way God made me." And should that fail they might declare, "Well, I didn't *ask* to be born!"

But excuses won't wash. They're just more "fig leaves" from the tree of self-righteousness. They didn't work for Adam and Eve, they won't work for us. We don't need anyone to inform us we're not altogether innocent—neither in conduct nor in thought. We *know* the difference between right and wrong, good and evil.

I was about five years old when a little friend and I got into my dad's trunk where he kept his cigars and cigarettes. I don't know how many cigarettes we smoked, but we topped them off with a cigar. Mom said when she came home from work, leaning against the porch with a cigarette between my little fingers, I greeted her with a, "*Hi, ya, mom!*"

I don't recall that dad ever told me to stay out of his trunk. But even at that young age I knew I shouldn't mess with his stuff. I guess I was just foolish enough to think he wouldn't know. But it wasn't long before my sins found me out.[134] That night as the family sat at supper I lay on a cot nearby, too sick to eat. Once dad looked over at me and asked, "Son, want a cigarette?" He chuckled as I rolled to the side of the cot and threw up.

I knew before I opened dad's trunk that it was wrong. So it is with us all. The devil doesn't make us do "it." The attraction to sin is ever present in the shadows of our hearts.[135] Satan merely provides idea and opportunity.

The foundation of sin is *I will*, and its instigator is Lucifer. The spiritual life of many is rooted in the worship of *I will*, rather than a love for the *I Am*.[136]

But God, through the prophet Isaiah, predicts the ultimate end of all those who live their life in obedience to the god of *self-will*.

> "How are you fallen from heaven, O Lucifer, son of the morning! How are you cut down to the ground, which did weaken the nations! For you have said in your heart, 'I will ascend into heaven. I will exalt my throne above the stars[137] of God! I will sit also upon the mount of the congregation, in the sides of the north. I will ascend above the heights of the clouds. I will be like the most High.' Yet you shall be brought down to hell, to the sides of the pit.
>
> "They that see you shall narrowly look upon you, and consider you, saying, 'Is this the man that made the earth to tremble, that did shake kingdoms; that made the world as a wilderness, and destroyed the cities thereof; that opened not the house of his prisoners?'"
>
> Isaiah 14:12–17

> Then shall he say also unto them on the left hand, "Depart from me, you cursed, into everlasting fire, prepared for the devil and his angels."
>
> Matthew 25:41

What those cigarettes did to my body, sin does to our spirit. Just as our physical bodies are not meant to operate on nicotine, alcohol and the like, neither is our spirit designed to run on sin.

The problem is that our sin nature deceives us into thinking we have the *right* to do what we do, that there's no harm in doing it, and we're offended when disciplined. Therefore, when injury does occur, rather than perpetrator, we claim to be the victim. But that excuse is poor camouflage, my friend, and truth sees right through it.

The Cross, The Lamb and Greater Love

Who crucified the Christ? Was it the Jew, the Roman, the Gentile? Or does it really matter? I have taught, and still hold to the position that no Roman soldier participated in the arrest of Jesus.[138] Never having found anyone who agreed, I began to think that maybe it was too trivial a thing to mention.

But one day after class a lady approached and, tears filling her eyes, thanked me. She said that as an Italian, she had been accused many times of being one of the people who had crucified Christ. At that moment I was convinced that no truth is too small or insignificant.

With that in mind, beginning with one of the most familiar verses of the Bible, we will forever put to rest the debate of who was responsible for what happened to Jesus.

> For God so loved the world, that He gave...
>
> John 3:16a

The Greek word for gave is, *didomi.* It is used in a very wide application, including commit, deliver (up), and strike with the palm of the hand.[139] When combined with other scripture, we begin to see the cross more clearly.

> Yet it pleased the Lord to bruise Him. He (God) has put Him (Jesus) to grief.[140]
>
> Isaiah 53:10a

Here the word for bruise is *daká,* meaning, to crumble; to bruise, beat or to break in pieces, crush, destroy, humble, oppress, smite (with the open hand).[141] With the added information we might read John 3:16 as, "For God loved the world so much, that He slapped, struck, beat to pieces, His only Son, that whosoever believes in Him[142] should not perish, but have everlasting life."

It is inconceivable that a father should treat his son so severely, but that's exactly what God did. Although man was His instrument, it was God who used their evil hearts.[143]

> And…they lifted up their voice to God with one accord, and said, "Lord, You are God, which has made heaven, and earth, and the sea, and all that in them is. Who by the mouth of Your servant David has said, 'Why did the heathen rage, and the people imagine vain things?'[144]
>
> "The kings of the earth stood up, and the rulers were gathered together against the Lord, and against His Christ. For of a truth against Your holy child Jesus, whom You have anointed, both Herod, and Pontius Pilate, with the Gentiles, and the people of Israel, were gathered together, for to do whatsoever Your hand and Your counsel determined before to be done."
>
> Acts 4:24–28

> But Peter, standing up with the eleven, lifted up his voice, and said unto them,…"You men of Israel, hear these words. Jesus of Nazareth, a man approved of God among you by miracles and wonders and signs, which God did by Him in the midst of you, as you yourselves also know, Him, being delivered by the determinate counsel and foreknowledge of God, you have taken, and by wicked hands have crucified and slain."
>
> Acts 2:14a, 22–23

So intense is God's hatred of evil, He rained down the full force of His judgment of sin upon His own Son until Jesus was hammered beyond recognition.

His visage[145] was so marred[146] more than any man, and His form[147]
more than the sons of men.

Isaiah 52:13–14

Why? Why would God do such a thing to His own Son? It was
for you, my friend. It was for me. Jesus Christ accepted the punishment for our sin so that we might go free. The cross of Christ was
much more than a place of execution; it was an altar of love.

"Greater love has no man than this," said Jesus, "that a man lay
down his life for his friends."

John 15:13

"Therefore does my Father love Me, because I lay down My life,
that I might take it again. No man takes it from Me, but I lay it
down of Myself."

John 10:17–18a

No Way Out

Whatever else Pontius Pilate might have been, he was no fool. He knew the Jews were using him as their pawn.[148] Three times he declared Jesus to be innocent.[149] The Gospel writers report that he sought desperately for a way to release Jesus while averting a riot.[150] In an effort to avoid passing the death sentence, he resorted to "teaching Jesus a lesson" and letting Him go.

> And Pilate, when he had called together the chief priests and the rulers and the people, said unto them, "You have brought this man unto me, as one that perverts the people, and, behold, I, having examined Him before you, have found no fault in this man touching those things whereof you accuse Him. No, nor yet Herod. For I sent you to him. And, lo, nothing worthy of death is done unto Him. I will therefore chastise[151] Him, and release Him."
>
> Luke 23:13–16

As bizarre as it may seem, Pilate's decision to scourge Jesus was a desperate attempt at saving His life.[152] Motivated by sympathy for Jesus and dislike for the Jewish religious leaders, he hoped to appease them by the flogging.

But Pilate was not in control. God had chosen His sacrificial lamb[153] before creation,[154] and Pilate was powerless to free Him. He was a reluctant participant in God's plan of salvation of man as revealed in the shadows of prophecy, even from the beginning.[155]

After the scourging he had Jesus brought again before the people.

> Then came Jesus forth, wearing the crown of thorns, and the purple robe. And Pilate said unto them, "Behold the man!"
>
> John 19:5

"Look at the man," he shouted. "*Look* at Him!" Surely they would be satisfied and let the man go. A close examination of the scriptures gives the feeling that Pilate was repulsed by the callousness of the Jewish leaders. Finally, in a last ditch effort, he turned to Jewish law.

> When Pilate saw that he could prevail nothing, but that rather a tumult[156] was made, he took water, and washed his hands before the multitude, saying, "I am innocent of the blood of this just person. See you to it."
>
> Matthew 27:24–24

The words, *to it*, are not in the original text, but were added in an effort to give clarity. Jewish law stated that if a murdered man was found between two cities and the murderer was unknown, the city nearest the man would bear the responsibility for his death.[157]

> And all the elders of that city, that are next unto the slain man, shall wash their hands over the [sacrificial] heifer that is beheaded in the valley. And they shall answer and say, "Our hands have not shed this blood, neither have our eyes seen it."
>
> Deuteronomy 21:6–7

Pilate then, washed his hands over God's sacrificial lamb, saying, "I am innocent of the blood of this just person. Look!"
How horrifying, and prophetic, was the response of the Jews.

> Then answered all the people, and said, "His blood be on us, and on our children."
>
> Matthew 27:25

Throughout the gospel accounts we see Jesus in absolute control of every situation.

> Then said Pilate unto Him, "Do you not speak to me? Know you

not that I have power[158] to crucify you, and have power to release you?"

Jesus answered, "You could have no power at all against Me, except it were given you from above."[159]

John 19:10–11a

Even His arrest required His permission.

Jesus therefore, knowing all things that should come upon Him, went forth, and said unto them, "Whom seek you?"

They answered Him, "Jesus of Nazareth."

Jesus said unto them, "I am."[160]

And Judas also, which betrayed Him, stood with them. As soon then as He had said unto them, "I am," they went backward, and fell to the ground.

John 18:4–6[161]

Jesus left no room for doubt that He, not man, was in charge.

Then Simon Peter having a sword drew it, and smote the high priest's servant, and cut off his right ear. The servant's name was Malchus.

John 18:10

Then said Jesus unto him, "Put up again your sword into his place: for all they that take the sword shall perish with the sword. Think you that I cannot now pray to My Father, and He shall presently give Me more than twelve legions of angels?"

Matthew 26:52–53

I once was asked to do something in relation to my job I thought not quite proper. It was not a bad thing, just a "good business practice." When I told my manager I could not comply, the subject was dropped and not mentioned again for over two years.

Then one day while walking past his office I saw him in conference with a man I had worked with at another company. The thought went through my mind that this man was my replacement. A few days later I was called into the manager's office and discharged.

Having been "forewarned," I was at peace. But my manager appeared uncomfortable at having to dismiss me and paid me twice the required severance pay. A short time later when the plant closed, I was already working with another company. My manager did not know it, but he had no choice in the matter. The decision had not been his to make, but God's.

And so it was with Pilate. Although history reports him to be evil and ruthless, with Jesus at least, he tried very hard to do the right thing.

Surface Relationships

Two families entered the restaurant where we were having lunch. It was obvious from their attire that they were of a Christian persuasion. As the men and one of the wives seated themselves, the second lady settled the children, then went to the counter to order their food. The children were well behaved but, as kids do, they were laughing and joking around. Just as the mother approached their table one of the boys, absorbed in telling a story, flung out his arms, hitting the trays and spilling the food to the floor.

Flustered and face flushed from embarrassment, the mother quickly knelt down and began scooping up the food with her hands. Going over to her I took her by her arm and raised her to her feet. "The manager will take care of that," I told her.

When I explained to the manager what had happened he immediately had the floor cleaned and the food replaced at no additional charge. The thing that struck me so was that not one of the other adults moved to help. In fact, they seemed oblivious to the whole incident.

Paul wrote that some people would have only a form of godliness, identifying them with those who were, "...lovers of their own selves, covetous, boasters, proud, blasphemers, disobedient to parents, unthankful, unholy, without natural affection, trucebreakers, false accusers, incontinent, fierce, despisers of those that are good, traitors, heady, high-minded, lovers of pleasures more than lovers of God. From such," he said, "turn away."[162]

Once a friend was trying very hard to quit smoking. Often she would call late at night asking for prayer. This went on for several weeks, but still she was hooked. Finally, I bought a pack of cigarettes and attached a note asking the Lord to please remove the craving. The next Sunday I placed the cigarettes on the church altar for our friend. As I was walking back to my seat, one after the other, three men put their arm around my shoulders promising to be praying for me. One said he understood—that he had gone through the same battle himself. They had assumed the problem was mine. The thought went through my mind, *Things aren't always as they seem.* It's important to understand that God is Creator and Master of reality. Satan is creator and master of illusion.

> There is a way which seems right unto a man, but the end thereof are the ways of death.
>
> Proverbs 14:12, 16:25

We must be careful not to believe everything we're told, even from those proclaiming to be God's special messengers. Paul warns the Corinthians,

> "Knowing this first, that no prophecy of the scripture is of any private[163] interpretation. For the prophecy came not in old time by the will of man, but holy men of God spoke as they were moved by the Holy Ghost.
>
> "But there were false prophets also among the people, even as there shall be false teachers among you, who privily shall bring in[164] damnable heresies,[165] even denying the Lord that bought them, and bring upon themselves swift destruction.
>
> "And many shall follow their pernicious[166] ways; by reason of whom the way of truth shall be evil spoken of. And through covetousness[167] shall they with feigned[168] words make merchandise of you: whose judgment now of a long time lingers not, and their damnation slumbers not."
>
> 2 Peter 1:20–2:3

Remember where we began? That there are those who teach that the black man is cursed of God and is to be the white man's servant? That is not truth, my friend. It's a damnable heresy. The bad news is that the great counterfeiter has come to steal, to kill and to destroy all whom he can.[169] The good news is, *But God.*

But God

In these two words lies the essence of the gospel.

*But God...*is rich in mercy, for His great love wherewith He loved us. (Ephesians 2:4)

*But God...*is longsuffering to us-ward, not willing that any should perish, but that all should come to repentance. (2 Peter 3:9)

*But God...*commended His love toward us, in that, while we were yet sinners, Christ died for us. (Romans 5:8)

But God...even when we were dead in sins, has made us alive together with Christ. (Ephesians 2:4a)

*But God...*so loved the world, that He gave His only begotten Son, that whosoever believes in Him should not perish, but have everlasting life. (John 3:16–17)

God did not send Jesus to condemn you, my friend,[170] but to save.[171] He came to destroy the works of the devil,[172] to call sinners to repentance,[173] that we might enjoy life in its fullness.[174]

He came to announce good news to the poor, to heal the brokenhearted, to proclaim freedom to the prisoner, and restoring of sight to the blind. To set at liberty them that are overcome by tragedy.[175]

Simply put, Jesus Christ came for *you,* and He came to lift you *up,* not put you down.

> "I waited patiently for the Lord," said David, "and He inclined unto me, and heard my cry. He brought me up also out of an horrible pit, out of the miry clay, and set my feet upon a rock, and

established my goings. And He has put a new song in my mouth, even praise unto our God. Many shall see it, and fear, and shall trust in the Lord.

"Blessed is that man that makes the Lord his trust, and respects not the proud, nor such as turn aside to lies."

Psalm 40:1–4

Although we have the ability to do as we please, we do not have the authority. We are not our own. We belong to God.[176] And as one song so aptly puts it, "God wants what He paid for."[177]

God loves you, my friend. He is not against you. He is for you. But not just you. He came for all mankind and all kind of men. However, like Adam and Eve in the beginning, we too attempt to hide from Him in a forest of religious rituals and to disguise our failures with leaves from the tree of self-righteousness.[178] Believers and unbelievers, righteousness and unrighteousness, light and darkness, reality and illusion, Christ and Satan, can not co-exist in peace.[179] Our difficulty is that God is holy and we are not.

We are all as an unclean thing, and all our righteousnesses are as filthy rags,[180] and we all do fade as a leaf; and our iniquities, like the wind, have taken us away.[181]

Isaiah 64:6

As light dispels darkness, so also the presence of Christ in our hearts removes all desire to sin.

Then spoke Jesus again unto them, saying, "I am the light of the world. He that follows Me shall not walk in darkness, but shall have the light of life."

John 8:12

My friend,

Whosoever is born of God does not commit sin;[182] for His seed remains in him: and he cannot sin, because he is born of God. In this the children of God are manifest,[183] and the children of the devil: whosoever does not righteousness is not of God, neither he that loves not his brother.[184]

For this is the message that you heard from the beginning, that we should love one another. Not as Cain, who was of that wicked one, and slew his brother. And wherefore slew he him? Because his own works were evil, and his brother's righteous.

1 John 3:9–12

In other words, if we harbor hate or contempt in our hearts for someone, or a people, we are not children of God but of Satan. John went on to explain that God's Word is truth, and if we know the truth, we can avoid Satan's deception.[185]

Unrighteousness is sin, and sin, as we have seen, ends in death. *But God...*not wanting us to perish,[186] sent His Word into the world in the form of a man.

Wherefore when He came into the world, He said, "Sacrifice and offering You would not,[187] but a body have You prepared Me."

Hebrews 10:5

And the Word was made flesh, and dwelt among us. And we beheld His glory, the glory as of the only begotten of the Father, full of grace [-fullness] and truth.

John 1:14

It was upon Him, His only Son, that God unleashed His wrath against sin.

"Surely He has borne our griefs, and carried our sorrows," wrote Isaiah. "Yet we did esteem Him stricken, smitten of God, and afflicted. But He was wounded for our transgressions, He was bruised for our iniquities. The chastisement of our peace was upon Him; and with His stripes we are healed."

Isaiah 53:4–5

Surely, my friend—*surely.*

Good News for the Sinner

God does not condemn us just because we sin. That's what sinners do. Fish swim, birds fly, sinners sin. Moreover, as sinners, we are already condemned.

> He that believes on Him is not condemned. But he that believes not is condemned already, because he has not believed in the name of the only begotten Son of God. And this is the condemnation, that light[188] is come into the world, and men loved darkness rather than light, because their deeds were evil.
>
> John 3:18–19

Therefore, Jesus did not come to condemn, but to save us.

> For God sent not His Son into the world to condemn the world; but that the world through Him might be saved.
>
> John 3:17

> For the Son of man is not come to destroy men's lives, but to save them.
>
> Luke 9:56a

He did not come to save us from sinning, but from our sin *nature*. Once our nature is changed, our *desire* to sin goes away.

> Therefore if any man be in Christ, he is a new creature.[189] Old things are passed away. Behold, all things are become new.
>
> 2 Corinthians 5:17

Sin is incontestable—and it's destructive—a deadly poison. We see evidence of it every day—experience it every day—wrestle with it in our own lives. Sin is offensive. And if it offends us, how much more a holy God?

> "Who shall ascend into the hill of the Lord?" asks the Psalmist. "Or who shall stand in His holy place?
>
> "He that has clean hands, and a pure heart," he goes on to explain, "who has not lifted up his soul unto vanity, nor sworn deceitfully."
>
> Psalm 24:3–4

How about you, my friend? Do you qualify? Are your hands clean? Do you have an absolutely pure heart? If you can't answer yes to all of the above then, guess what—you need an attorney to defend you with the Father, and that One is Jesus Christ.[190]

Take me for instance. I was always a very good liar but I was never a successful liar. I don't recall ever getting away with anything. Not the time I tried opening my sister's delicate little locket with my teeth, nor the time I dismantled her new doll and couldn't put it back together. (A note to young, inexperienced sinners. Under the bed is *not* a secure place to conceal your "experiments.") Somehow dad always knew. To hear him tell it I must have emerged from the womb lying.

When I was a little guy, kitchens had bins built under the counters for storing stuff like flour. Evidently flour was fun to play in because I was told many times, "Bobby! Stay out of the flour bin!"

Dad told of the day that he came home to find little white hand and foot prints all over the place. "Son," he asked. "Have you been in the flour bin?" "No sir!"

I never did own up to that little caper. The last time it was mentioned I was in my sixties. I had looked my dad straight in the eye and said, "Dad. I did *not* get into that flour bin." And we laughed together.

How about you? Ever told a lie? Not even a little "white" one? Never lost your temper or become unduly impatient with someone?

Never criticized or belittled or, "poked fun" at anyone to make them feel small?

We may be good compared to some others, but none of us can measure up to the goodness of God. Consequently we all have sinned,[191] and somehow, the Father of fathers always knows. But there is Good News![192] God is in the sinner reclamation business.[193] He transforms sinners like us into saints, just like the caterpillar into the butterfly.[194] He created us; He can recreate us.

> If we confess[195] our sins,[196] He is faithful and just to forgive us our sins, and to cleanse us from all unrighteousness.
>
> 1 John 1:9

> "Husbands," writes Paul, "love your wives, even as Christ also loved the church, and gave Himself for it. That He might sanctify and cleanse it with the washing of water by the word. That He might present it to Himself a glorious church, not having spot, or wrinkle, or any such thing, but that it should be holy and without blemish."
>
> Ephesians 5:25–27

Adam and Eve tried to cover their guilt with leaves. We try other gimmicks. This may come as a bit of a shock, my friend, but although they may make us more acceptable to others, all the colognes, after-shaves, perfumes, deodorants and soaps, wigs, face lifts and plastic surgery operations in the world can never remove the offence of sin from our hearts. And rehabilitation won't cut it. We need new hearts. And for that, we have to go back to the manufacturer.

Beginning Again for the First Time

Late one evening, a Jewish religious official named Nicodemus struck up a conversation with Jesus.

"We know You're a teacher come from God," he said. "For no man can do these miracles that You do, except God be with him."

Jesus cut through all the pomp and pageantry, legalism and liturgy, ritual and religion, and spoke straight to his heart.

"I tell you the truth," He said. "Unless a man is born again he can not see the kingdom of God."

"How can a man be born when he is old?" asked Nicodemus. "Can he enter the second time into his mother's womb, and be born?"

Jesus answered, "Verily, verily, I say unto you, except a man be born of water and of the Spirit, he cannot enter into the kingdom of God. That which is born of the flesh is flesh, and that which is born of the Spirit is spirit.[197] Marvel not that I said unto you, you must be born again. The wind blows where it lists,[198] and you hear the sound thereof, but can not tell whence it comes, and where it goes. So is every one that is born of the Spirit."

Nicodemus answered and said unto Him, "How can these things be?"

> Jesus answered and said unto him, "Are you a master[199] of Israel, and know not these things?"
>
> John 3:1–12

Nicodemus was a man of prominence among the Jews. To attain to his position, he had to be thoroughly knowledgeable in his religion. But this *born again* thing confused him, as it does many today.

Jesus was saying that, when we are born into the world, our spirits are alienated from the things of God,[200] being descendants of Adam and Eve. Apple trees produce apples. Grapevines produce grapes. Sinners produce sinners. Consequently, since Adam and Eve disobeyed God, we, being of their seed, are the children of disobedience by virtue of our heritage.[201]

The word *again* in the phrase, "born again," is from the Greek word, *anothen.* Its primary meaning is, *from above.* Just as we are born into this world, so also we must be born into God's world. There is simply no other way.

God is a Spirit.[202] Therefore, in order to communicate and fellowship with Him, our spirit must be made alive as well as our flesh—we must be born from above. Not once again physically, but once for the first time spiritually. Just as we were conceived physically by the seed of our earthly father, so must we be conceived spiritually by the seed of the heavenly Father.

The picture is clear. Just as man has seed within himself to produce natural children, so God has seed in Himself to produce spiritual children.

> "Now the parable is this," said Jesus. "The seed is the word of God."
>
> Luke 8:11

> "Being born again,"[203] said Peter, "not of corruptible seed, but of incorruptible, by the Word of God, which[204] lives and abides for ever."
>
> 1 Peter 1:23

There is no other remedy for the sin nature—it must be rooted out and replaced with God's nature. Without His Spirit we cannot enter,[205] or even *see*[206] His kingdom. That's why the natural man does not understand the things of God.

> The natural man receives not the things of the Spirit of God: for they are foolishness unto him: neither can he know them, because they are spiritually discerned.
>
> 1 Corinthians 2:14

Contrary to what many believe, not every one is God's child.

> "Now this I say, brethren," wrote Paul, "that flesh and blood cannot inherit the kingdom of God."
>
> 1 Corinthians 15:50a

> They which are the children of the flesh, these are not the children of God.
>
> Romans 9:8a

Only those who share God's Spirit are His children.

> For if you live after the flesh, you shall die: but if you through the Spirit do mortify the deeds of the body, you shall live. For as many as are led by the Spirit of God, they are the sons of God. For you have not received the spirit of bondage again to fear; but you have received the Spirit of adoption, whereby we cry, Abba, Father. The Spirit itself bears witness with our spirit, that we are the children of God.
>
> Romans 8:13–16

But everyone *can* be.

> He came unto His own, and His own received Him not. But as many as received Him, to them gave He power[207] to become the sons[208] of God, even to them that believe on His name. Which were born, not of blood, nor of the will of the flesh, nor of the will of man, but of God.
>
> John 1:11–13

We all have inherited Adam's traits. It was from his attitude that sprang all death, all sicknesses, all diseases, all wars, all drunkenness, fornication, adultery, incest—all evil. It is from *our* attitudes that they continue. To sin is in our very nature. We *must* be born again.

Choosing a Father

When God created, He put within each created thing the seed for producing others of its own kind,[209] including man.

> So God created man in His own image. In the image of God created He him. Male and female created He them. And God blessed them. And God said unto them, "Be fruitful, and multiply, and replenish[210] the earth..."
>
> Genesis 1:27–28a,b

Only by man sowing his seed into the womb of woman can this mandate be accomplished. All other sexual relationships are a corruption of God's design and yield painful consequences.

> And likewise also the men, leaving the natural use of the woman, burned in their lust one toward another; men with men working that which is unseemly, and receiving in themselves that recompense[211] of their error[212] which was meet.[213]
>
> Romans 1:27

But God does not need the services of man to produce more people. When John the Baptist saw many of the religious Jews coming to his baptism, he challenged them, saying,

> "Think not to say within yourselves, we have Abraham to our father. For I say unto you, that God is able of these stones to raise up children unto Abraham."
>
> Matthew 3:9

Therefore, the marriage relationship carries a much greater responsibility than just the bearing of children. It is a *type*,[214] pointing to a higher purpose. It reveals God's longing for children of His own. Not those born of man, but those fathered of Himself[215]—those who bear His nature. And the marriage relationship illustrates how this is accomplished.

God's design is for one man and one woman, committed and faithful. That is why a holy God will tolerate no form of sexual immorality.

Concerning divorce Jesus said,

> "It has been said, 'Whosoever shall put away his wife, let him give her a writing of divorcement.' But I say unto you, that whosoever shall put away his wife, saving for the cause of fornication, causes her to commit adultery: and whosoever shall marry her that is divorced commits adultery."
>
> Matthew 5:31–32

The Biblical justification for divorce is not adultery alone, but fornication. The Greek word for fornication is *porneia* from which we get our English word, pornography, and includes any and all forms of illicit or unnatural sex acts, or the *viewing* thereof.

We are clearly warned in Galatians 6:7–8,

> Be not deceived; God is not mocked: for whatsoever a man sows, that shall he also reap. For he that sows to his flesh shall of the flesh reap corruption; but he that sows to the Spirit shall of the Spirit reap life everlasting.

and again in Romans 1:18,

> For the wrath[216] of God is revealed from heaven against all ungodliness and unrighteousness of men, who hold the truth in unrighteousness.

God spoke categorically in Isaiah 55:10–11 when He said,

> "For as the rain comes down, and the snow from heaven, and returns not there, but waters the earth, and makes it bring forth

and bud, that it may give seed to the sower, and bread to the eater, so shall My word be that goes forth out of My mouth. It shall not return unto Me void, but it shall accomplish that which I please, and it shall prosper in the thing whereto I sent it."

Isaiah 55:10–11

For any seed to thrive it must be sown into good ground.[217] God found good ground for His Seed in a young virgin girl named Mary.

And Mary said, "Behold the handmaid of the Lord. Be it unto me according to Your word."

Luke 1:38a

Even though Mary understood the danger she faced when discovered to be pregnant,[218] she chose to believe and obey God. And so was born Jesus of Nazareth. God's Word, nourished in the womb of woman, became "that Holy Thing" spoken of by the angel[219]—fully God in Spirit, fully man in body.[220] The only one of His kind, Jesus now becomes the seed from which a new people would emerge.

And Jesus answered them, saying, "The hour is come, that the Son of man should be glorified.[221] Verily, verily, I say unto you, except a grain of wheat fall into the ground and die, it abides alone. But if it die, it brings forth much fruit."[222]

John 12:23–24

In James 1:18 we read,

"Of His own will begot He us with the word of truth, that we should be a kind of firstfruits of His creatures."[223]

and again,

"But now is Christ risen from the dead, and become the firstfruits of them that slept."

1 Corinthians 15:20

Of those born of God, Peter writes,

> "But you are a chosen generation, a royal priesthood, an holy nation, a peculiar[224] people...Which in time past were not a people, but are now the people of God."
>
> 1 Peter 2:9a-10a

This new species would be made up of peoples of all nations, ethnic groups and colors.

> Then Peter opened his mouth, and said, "Of a truth I perceive that God is no respecter of persons. But in every nation he that fears Him, and works righteousness, is accepted with Him."
>
> Acts 10:34–35

When we accept Jesus into our hearts, we receive the *seed* of God's nature, that is, His Spirit of

> ...love, joy, peace, longsuffering, gentleness, goodness, faith, meekness, temperance.
>
> Galatians 5:22–23a

But it isn't enough just to be conceived of God. The seed must take root and grow. There is a world of difference between the *seed* in us and *Christ* in us. Not all the seed sown by God survives.[225] As with any seed, it must be nourished.[226] Just as we are trained in the things of this world, so must we be instructed in the things of God. That's what John meant when he wrote that those who receive the seed[227] are given the ability to become children of God.[228]

God shows no favoritism. He cares for all men equally. His invitation is given to everyone, regardless of their size, shape or color.

> "Come unto Me, all you that labor and are heavy laden," said Jesus, "and I will give you rest."[229]
>
> Matthew 11:28

> "All that the Father gives Me shall come to Me. And him that comes to Me I will in no wise cast out. And this is the will of Him that sent Me, that every one which sees the Son, and believes on

Him, may have everlasting life. And I will raise him up at the
last day."

John 6:37, 40

Although the invitation is all-inclusive,[230] only those produced by
His Seed[231] become His family.[232] How about you, my friend? Are
you good ground for eternal life?—for a love relationship with your
Creator?

If you have not yet met the person of Jesus, do it now. He longs for
a personal, intimate, relationship with you. The only thing wanting
is your invitation.

"Behold," He calls. "I stand at the door, and knock. If any man
[one] hear My voice, and open the door, I will come in to Him,
and will sup with him, and he with Me."

Revelation 3:20

Dear friend, just now, if you "hear" Him at the door of your heart,
lay aside the book and let Him in, won't you? *Now* is the accepted
time—*now* is the day of salvation.[233] You may say something as simple as, "God, I want to be Your child." If you are sincere, you will
immediately be welcomed into His family. Only then is one qualified to pray, "Our Father, which art in heaven."[234]

If you prayed that prayer, listen. Can you hear them? There is great
rejoicing going on in heaven because of your decision. Jesus said,

"I say unto you, that likewise joy shall be in heaven over one sinner that repents, more than over ninety and nine just persons,
which need no repentance."

Luke 15:7

Even God is singing.

The Lord your God in the midst of you is mighty. He will save.
He will rejoice over you with joy. He will rest in his love. He will
joy over you with singing.

Zephaniah 3:17

On the other hand, we have the freedom to choose Satan if we wish, and many do.

> "You are of your father the devil," charged Jesus, "and the lusts of your father you will do. He was a murderer from the beginning, and abode not in the truth, because there is no truth in him. When he speaks a lie, he speaks of his own. For he is a liar, and the father of it."
>
> John 8:44

> Jesus answered them, "Have not I chosen you twelve, and one of you is a devil?" He spoke of Judas Iscariot, the son of Simon: for he it was that should betray Him, being one of the twelve.
>
> John 6:70–71

You may not be aware of doing so, but you will choose one or the other.

> "He that is not with Me," said Jesus, "is against Me. And he that gathers not with Me scatters abroad."
>
> Matthew 12:30

New Heart, New Start

The reason we tend to scorn others is because our own hearts have been corrupted by sin. Like King David, we need a new heart.[235] Although Ezekiel 36:24–27 is addressed specifically to the nation of Israel, it reveals God's work in the individual in *type*[236]—it unravels the mystery of "Christ in you."[237]

> "For I will take you from among the heathen," said God, "and gather you out of all countries, and will bring you into your own land. Then will I sprinkle clean water upon you, and you shall be clean from all your filthiness, and from all your idols, will I cleanse you.

> "A new heart also will I give you, and a new spirit will I put within you. And I will take away the stony heart out of your flesh, and I will give you an heart of flesh. And I will put My Spirit within you, and cause you to walk in My statutes, and you shall keep My judgments, and do them."[238]

When we accept God's work in us, we become a brand new creation. Not one that has been reconditioned, but one that has never before existed.[239]

With a new heart comes a new nature.[240] We can start over, my friend. Regardless of what lies in our past—it's *past*. We can forget our regrets and look to the future.[241] But God requires our whole heart. What He says to the church of the Laodiceans He says to us as well.

> "I know your works, that you are neither cold nor hot. I would you were cold or hot. So then because you are lukewarm, and neither cold nor hot, I will spew[242] you out of my mouth."
>
> Revelation 3:15–16

We must crucify our "old man,"[243]

> "This I say therefore, and testify in the Lord," writes Paul, "that you henceforth walk not as other Gentiles walk, in the vanity of their mind, that you put off concerning the former conversation[244] the old man,[245] which is corrupt according to the deceitful lusts; and be renewed in the spirit of your mind. And that you put on the new man,[246] which after God is created in righteousness and true holiness."
>
> Ephesians 4:17, 22–24

and be wholly faithful to our new. Jesus said,

> "If you love Me keep My commandments."
>
> John 14:15

He went on to add,

> "If a man love Me, he will keep My words. And My Father will love him, and We will come unto him, and make our abode with him. He that loves Me not keeps not My sayings. And the word which you hear is not Mine, but the Father's which sent Me."
>
> John 14:23–24

The evidence of a new heart is a changed life. Paul writes,

> "They that are Christ's have crucified the flesh with the affections[247] and lusts.[248] If we live in the Spirit, let us also walk in the Spirit. Let us not be desirous of vain glory,[249] provoking[250] one another, envying one another."
>
> Galatians 5:24–26

Team Spirit

The year I joined the baseball team our High School had just purchased new uniforms—and I wanted one. I mean, I *really* wanted one. But being a freshman and new to the team I had to settle for one that was older and a little threadbare.

That first year I played in only five games, but in every game I gave it all I had. Regardless of where the ball was hit, I backed the play. I pounded the pocket of my glove until it was paper-thin so the ball would stick when caught. I sharpened my "batting eye," practiced fielding, quick "start-stop" running—everything I could to make first string the next year, and I succeeded. With hard work and a love for the game, by the end of the eleventh grade I was in line for a scholarship at a small college. It wasn't that I was that good, far from it. Any success I had came because, somewhere between the eighth and ninth grades, I had caught the *spirit* of baseball.

When our son was just learning to play baseball, I was helping one day with little league practice. My job was to umpire behind the pitcher. Just a little guy, one boy was having trouble in getting the ball even close to the plate.

Not wanting him to become discouraged, I gave the calls as much room as I could without being too apparent. But he just couldn't quite get the ball to the plate. So batter after batter was walked. Finally, he turned and, looking at me with tears welling up in his big sad eyes asked, "Whose side are you on anyway?"

God is on your side. He wants you to make the team.

"The Lord is not slack concerning His promise, as some men count slackness," writes Peter, "but is longsuffering to us-ward, not willing that any should perish, but that all should come to repentance."

2 Peter 3:9

He is cheering for you.

"For I know the thoughts that I think toward you," says the Lord. "Thoughts of peace, and not of evil, to give you an expected end."[251]

Jeremiah 29:11

He *believes* in you, and has provided everything you need to succeed.

"What shall we then say to these things?" asks Paul. "If God be for us, who can be against us? He that spared not His own Son, but delivered Him up for us all, how shall He not with Him also freely give us all things?"

Romans 8:31–32

Just as I was not born with a love for baseball, neither are we born with a thought for God. The truth is that, in the beginning, none of us know anything about Him. But within each of us is the knowledge that there is a God,[252] and we have a stirring in our spirit to know Him. As a result, not knowing what God is like, men invent gods of their own imaginations. Hence, the thousands of religions, cults and schisms.

But God is not about religion or ritual.[253] He's about relationship.[254] So passionate is His desire for intimacy with you and me that He indicted, condemned and executed sin in His own Son for our transgressions.

...and the Lord has laid on Him the iniquity of us all.

Isaiah 53:6b

Moreover, through the apostle Peter, He invites us to share His own unique nature.

"Grace and peace be multiplied unto you through the knowledge of God, and of Jesus our Lord, according as His divine power has given unto us all things that pertain unto life and godliness, through the knowledge of Him that has called us to glory and virtue.

"Whereby are given unto us exceeding great and precious promises, that by these you might be partakers of the divine[255] nature,[256] having escaped the corruption that is in the world through lust."

2 Peter 1:2–4

Not everyone who does the religious "stuff" makes the team. Jesus warns,

"Not every one that says unto Me, 'Lord, Lord,' shall enter into the kingdom of heaven; but he that does the will of My Father which is in heaven. Many will say to Me in that day, 'Lord, Lord, have we not prophesied in Your name? And in Your name have cast out devils? And in Your name done many wonderful works?'

"And then will I profess unto them, 'I never knew you. Depart from Me, you that work iniquity.'"

Matthew 7:21–23

Consequently, just because we may play the game does not make us a part of His team.

"You hypocrites!" said Jesus. "Well did Isaiah prophesy of you, saying, 'This people draws nigh unto Me with their mouth, and honors Me with their lips, but their heart is far from Me.' But in vain they do worship Me, teaching for doctrines the commandments of men."

Matthew 15:7–9

I and a friend once coached a little league baseball team. One fifteen-year-old was a natural born athlete, our own personal "Mickey Mantle." We were at the ballpark preparing for our fourth game when he came strolling by—in a suit—to tell us goodbye. He was quitting the team. He had lost his spirit for baseball to a pretty, fourteen-year-old girl and we lost our star player to the lust of the flesh and the lust of the eyes.

Amos 3:3 asks, "Can two walk together, except they be agreed?" From our own experiences we know the answer is, of course not! If we attempt to play the game of baseball by the rules of another sport we would not make the team. We must be in harmony with the other players.

Life is God's idea, my friend. It's His game, and He will not alter the rules just to accommodate us.[257] Consequently, if we refuse to play by His rules, guess what? No uniform.

French Fries and Jesus

Our pastor tells of a little girl who had truly caught the concept of Christ in us. One day while eating, as a French fry dropped down into her little tummy, she suddenly exclaimed, "Oops! I just hit Jesus on the head." The things of God are pretty simple for a child's mind. But as we grow older, it seems we also grow more skeptical—or perhaps, *arrogant*.

> Because that, when they knew God, they glorified Him not as God, neither were thankful, but became vain in their imaginations, and their foolish heart was darkened.
>
> Professing themselves to be wise, they became fools, and changed the glory of the uncorruptible God into an image made like to corruptible man, and to birds, and four footed beasts, and creeping things.
>
> Romans 1:21–23

> There is a generation that are pure in their own eyes, and yet is not washed from their filthiness.
>
> Proverbs 30:12

When Nicodemus asked, "How can a man be born when he is old," Jesus compared the Spiritual birth to the unseen wind.[258] But when Mary asked the same question,[259] Gabriel explained,

> "The Holy Ghost[260] shall come upon you, and the power of the

Highest shall overshadow you. Therefore also that Holy Thing which shall be born of you shall be called the Son of God."

Luke 1:31–35

Since God is holy,[261] and He is a spirit,[262] Gabriel is saying that God Himself would "come upon" Mary. Although Jesus existed in the beginning with God, He existed as God's Word[263] and not with a body.

And so Gabriel came to Mary with the message, "God said."[264] When Mary accepted what God said, His Spirit "came upon" her and what God said took root in her womb, and a human embryo was conceived.

> Then Joseph her husband, being a just man, and not willing to make her a public example, was minded to put her away[265] privately.[266] But while he thought on these things, behold, the angel of the Lord appeared unto him in a dream, saying, "Joseph, you son of David, fear not to take unto you Mary your wife. For that which is conceived in her is of the Holy Ghost. And she shall bring forth a son, and you shall call His name Jesus, for He shall save His people from their sins."
>
> Now all this was done, that it might be fulfilled which was spoken of the Lord by the prophet, saying, "Behold, a virgin shall be with child, and shall bring forth a son, and they shall call His name Emmanuel, which being interpreted is, 'God with us.'"

Matthew 1:19–23

In this Holy Thing, God would dwell on earth among men.

> "Beware," warned Paul, "lest any man spoil you through philosophy and vain deceit, after the tradition of men, after the rudiments of the world, and not after Christ. For in Him dwells all the fullness of the Godhead[267] bodily."[268]

Colossians 2:8–9

The birth of Jesus is a physical depiction of the spiritual birth—of Christ in us. Just as with Mary in the natural, God comes to us through His Word and His Spirit.

So then faith comes by hearing, and hearing by the word of God.

Romans 10:17

Jesus answered, "Verily, verily, I say unto you, except a man be born of water[269] and of the Spirit,[270] he cannot enter into the kingdom of God."

John 3:5

When we believe and accept what God says,[271] His Spirit will "come upon" and "lie over" us to impregnate us with His incorruptible seed, His Word.[272] As it is physically with man and wife, so it is spiritually with God and man.

"Wives," wrote Paul, "submit yourselves unto your own husbands."

Ephesians 5:22

"Husbands, love your wives."

Ephesians 5:25

"For this cause shall a man leave his father and mother, and shall be joined[273] unto his wife, and they two shall be one flesh. This is a great mystery, but I speak concerning Christ and the church."

Ephesians 5:31–32

Here Paul is using the analogy of husband and wife to illustrate a greater truth, the relationship God desires with us through His Son. Jesus became God with us[274] in order that we might come to know God personally, intimately.

Jesus said unto him, "Have I been so long time with you, and yet have you not known Me, Philip? He that has seen Me has seen the Father. And how say you then, 'Show us the Father?'"

John 14:9

John testifies that he and the other apostles had such a relationship, and that their passion is that we enjoy that same closeness with

Jesus, and with one another. The whole of Christianity is wrapped up in John's one single statement,

> "That which was[275] from the beginning, which we have heard, which we have seen with our eyes, which we have looked upon, and our hands have handled, of the Word of life; (For the Life was manifested, and we have seen It,[276] and bear witness, and show unto you that Eternal Life, which was[277] with the Father, and was manifested unto us.)

> That which we have seen and heard declare we unto you, that you also may have fellowship with us. And truly our fellowship is with the Father, and with His Son Jesus Christ."
>
> 1 John 1:1–3

When Christ is *in* us, He is part *of* us, and we are a part of Him.[278] Therefore, if you have accepted Christ as your Lord and Savior, remember to chew your food thoroughly. When you swallow, you just might "hit Jesus on His head."

A House Divided

Lucifer was one of God's princes. He was very wise and eminently beautiful.[279] It is thought by many that his responsibilities included leading the worship of God in heaven.[280] He was adorned with precious gems and gold[281] and was exceeding wealthy.[282] But pride entered his heart.[283] He wanted to be like God.[284]

> "Your heart was lifted up because of your beauty," charged God. "You have corrupted your wisdom by reason of your brightness."[285]
>
> Ezekiel 28:17a

God's house was now divided. Conflict was inevitable. God must deal with rebellion else His kingdom would be in chaos.[286] And so Lucifer was judged, found guilty, and sentenced. And although he still had access to God,[287] one day he will be banished forever and utterly destroyed.

> And there was war in heaven. Michael and his angels fought against the dragon. And the dragon fought and his angels, and prevailed not. Neither was their place found any more in heaven. And the great dragon was cast out, that old serpent, called the devil, and Satan, which deceives the whole world. He was cast out into the earth, and his angels[288] were cast out with him.
>
> Revelation 2:7–9

It will happen exactly as God predicted in Ezekiel 28:16–17b.

"By the multitude of your merchandise they have filled the midst of you with violence, and you have sinned. Therefore I will cast you as profane out of the mountain of God. And I will destroy you, O covering cherub,[289] from the midst of the stones of fire."

And the devil that deceived them was cast into the lake of fire and brimstone, where the beast and the false prophet are, and shall be tormented day and night for ever and ever.

Revelation 20:10

In the beginning, man reflected the image of God and they shared a closeness. But as with Lucifer, Adam rebelled and their fellowship was broken. Once again, God's kingdom divided. No longer did Adam reflect the image of his Creator, but that of his adversary, Satan.

There is a way that seems right, but leads to death.[290] Adam had a choice—the tree of life, or the tree of the knowledge of good and evil.[291] Unfortunately he made the wrong choice, thereby setting the course for all of mankind. He would now produce children in his own likeness, a sinner.

And Adam lived an hundred and thirty years, and begat a son in his own likeness, after his image; and called his name Seth.

Genesis 5:3

Once Adam had been excited in his wife.[292] But now Satan had entered his heart.[293] In an attempt to excuse his own sin, he deliberately offered her up as a sacrifice to God's judgment.

And He (God) said, "Who told you that you were naked? Have you eaten of the tree, whereof I commanded you that you should not eat?"

And the man said, "The woman whom You gave to be with me, she gave me of the tree, and I did eat."

But before Eve sinned, Adam had already sinned in his heart.

Wherefore, as by one man sin entered into the world, and death by sin; and so death passed upon all men, for that all have sinned.

Romans 5:12

He had succumbed to the stimulation of lust and pride.[294]

The Bible records that as Eve was being tempted, Adam was there with her.[295] God had sternly warned that anyone eating from the forbidden tree would surely, without a doubt, die. Yet he stood silently by—watching. Was God telling them the truth? Would Eve really die?

And so the man's relationship with his wife was broken as well as his relationship with God. Whereas initially man and woman had walked in harmony as co-administrators of creation, now they would compete for control.

> Unto the woman He said, "I will greatly multiply your sorrow and your conception. In sorrow you shall bring forth children. And your desire shall be to your husband, and he shall rule over you."
>
> Genesis 3:16

A more clear understanding would be, "You shall desire to rule over your husband, but he shall rule over you."[296] Thus arose contention between man and woman.

If Lucifer could not be a god, then he would destroy God's kingdom by dividing His people. They in turn would destroy one another and God's dream would die. In one man Lucifer had sown the seed of rebellion and found him to be good ground. As a result, Adam betrayed his wife and his first son murdered his younger. That's why God hates division, my friend. His nature is unity. Division invites conflict—strife—destruction.

Jesus said He spoke only the things God told Him to say.[297] Therefore, we can know that God's desire is for all mankind to be as one. Listen closely as He prays for you and me.

> "That they all may be one, as You, Father, are in Me, and I in You. That they also may be one in Us, that the world may believe that You have sent Me. And the glory which You gave Me I have given them, that they may be one, even as We are one.
>
> "I in them, and You in Me, that they may be made perfect[298] in one, and that the world may know that You have sent Me, and have loved them, as You have loved Me."
>
> John 17:21–23

Without harmony among its citizens, God's kingdom, [and His church], would be as the world is today. Therefore, all one has to do to grieve God and to please Lucifer is to create division, strife or discord. So it is with a kingdom or a nation. So it is with a marriage or family.

Breakfast by Candlelight

Being a bit of a romantic, I thought one day to surprise my wife with a "breakfast by candlelight." There's a small drive-in restaurant just around the corner from our house where they serve a great breakfast. We have eaten there many times.

I told the owner my idea and asked his permission to burn the candles. The next morning I informed my wife I was going out and would be back in about ten minutes. I asked her to please be ready to go as soon as I returned. She said, OK, and I left to set the tablecloth, light the candles and order our breakfast. The cook began our food and I rushed home to get my lovely, obedient, bride—but she wasn't ready. She was dawdling, doing that woman stuff that seems to us guys to take forever.

So I asked her to, "Come *on*, let's *go!*" And she says, "*Wait* a minute." And I say, "I *asked* you to be ready when I got *back*. Let's *go!* Get in the car!"

And she says some other stuff, and I say some other stuff, and by the time we headed for the restaurant, we both were so angry we weren't speaking. Nor did we speak throughout our romantic breakfast by candlelight. I'm sure that while Lucifer was howling with delight, God was going, "Oh, no. Not *again.*"

The current divorce rate among couples is at fifty percent and rising. That includes Christians, who are supposed to love one another. In Jesus' day, some Jews believed divorce was permissible for any reason, including such things as poor cooking. Man has not changed much since those times.

Some years ago a woman wrote to Ann Landers' advice column that she wanted to divorce her husband. The reason she gave was that her husband rubbed his feet together when sleeping, and the noise kept her awake.

To paraphrase an earlier scripture,

> If a man say, "I love God," but does not treat his wife (or husband) with kindness and respect,[299] he is a liar. For he that does not show kindness toward his wife or husband whom he has seen, how can he respect God whom he has not seen? And this commandment have we from Him, that he who loves God love his wife, (or husband) also.
>
> 1 John 4:20–21

Each day, each moment, we have decisions to make. We have been given the same choices as God allowed Adam and Eve. How will we decide? Do we follow the destroyer—or the life giver? And we will follow one or the other.

Kicking Down Walls

It is important to note that, although Adam had sinned, still God kept their appointed time of fellowship.[300] Therefore, God did not reject Adam because of his sin, Adam rejected God because of his consciousness of sin.

> And he (Adam) said, "I heard Your voice in the garden, and I was afraid, because I was naked, and I hid myself."
>
> Genesis 3:10

Inside Israel's tabernacle were two notable partitions, separated by a veil—the Holy Place and the Holy of Holies. The veil symbolized the separation between man and God. God hated that barrier and sent His only Son with instructions to tear it down. Out of His great love for mankind, God opened a way into the Holy of Holies through His Son.[301]

> "I am the door," said Jesus. "By Me, if any man enter in, he shall be saved, and shall go in, and out, and find pasture."
>
> John 10:9

He is not *a* door, but *the* door—the *only* door. There is no other way to God but through the Son. Jesus declared that He alone was the way, the truth and the life. No man, He said, can approach the Father except through Himself.[302]

The message of the Bible is clear. To reach God, we must go through Jesus.

> He that believes on the Son has everlasting life. And he that believes not the Son shall not see life; but the wrath of God abides on him.
>
> John 3:36

It was in Him that God destroyed that dividing wall He so hated.

> But now in Christ Jesus, you who sometimes were far off are made near by the blood of Christ. For He is our peace, Who has made both[303] one,[304] and has broken down the middle wall of partition between us.
>
> Ephesians 2:13–14

And so God allowed mankind to tear open the door to salvation—the body of Christ.

> Having therefore, brethren, boldness to enter into the holiest by the blood of Jesus, by a new and living way, which He has consecrated for us, through the veil, that is to say, His flesh.
>
> Hebrews 10:19–20

Jesus offered no defense or resistance to His accusers,

> He was oppressed, and He was afflicted, yet He opened not His mouth. He is brought as a lamb to the slaughter, and as a sheep before her shearers is dumb, so He opened not His mouth.
>
> Isaiah 53:7[305]

because He was taking our punishment, and we all are guilty. It should have been my back under that Roman scourge—it should have been yours. The pain and shame He endured was meant for me—it was meant for you.[306]

None of us have justification for thinking ourselves better than another, for no one has ever, nor can ever, measure up to God.[307] Oh, my friend, God does not build walls to keep us out. He tears them down to let us in.

And, behold, the veil of the temple was rent in twain from the top
to the bottom; and the earth did quake, and the rocks rent.

Matthew 27:51)

Satan has deceived us into writing across the veil "Warning! Keep
out! God will destroy you." But God has written in the blood of His
only Son, "I love you. Please, please, come in."[308]

Satan's work is to separate man from his Creator. Jesus came to
destroy his works,[309] and He completed what He came to do,[310]
opening the way into the presence of God. Jesus Himself invites us
to drink from the wellspring of eternal life.

"I, Jesus, have sent My angel to testify unto you these things in the
churches. I am the root and the offspring of David, and the bright
and morning star. And the Spirit and the bride say, 'Come.' And
let him that hears say, 'Come.' And let him that is athirst come.
And whosoever will, let him take the water of life freely."

Revelation 22:16–17

The invitation is not to you only, or your family, or race, or nation.
But to all men, whosoever will.

The writer to the Hebrews asks,

"How shall we escape, if we neglect so great salvation; which at
the first began to be spoken by the Lord, and was confirmed unto
us by them that heard Him."

Hebrews 2:3

We can't, my friend. So the wise thing to do would be, don't
neglect so great salvation.[311] We have been inundated by the reports
of others—in the Bible we have the report of God. The question we
must answer is, who's report will we believe?[312]

My Momma's Baby Boy

As a four-year-old, I was playing one day with my wagon in a field near our home. Suddenly I felt "the call" and began running hard for the house. When mom saw me heading for home without the wagon she hollered, "Bobby! Don't leave your wagon!"

"But, *mom!* I hafta go to th' *bath*room!"

"I told you to go back and get that wagon!"

"But *Mom…!*" By this time I was dancing around pretty lively.

"Bobby! You know what your daddy said! You get that wagon back in this yard *right this minute!*"

So, back I went. And as I went, I went, and the urgency of the moment passed.

Now, my mom was not trying to be mean spirited. She just didn't have all the facts. Had she understood, the wagon would not have been an issue.

Although a little crude, that experience sometimes reflects our spiritual us. Even when our intentions are honorable we sometimes fall a little short of a proper attitude or behavior. Accepting Jesus as Savior is not our final destination, it's merely the beginning. He will be Lord as well. Consequently, after the new birth comes the training, the discipline, the maturing.

As a baby Christian, I "knew it all." You know the type. I was a real pain to a lot of folks. But one lady began praying for me. So while I was busy soiling my spiritual diapers, she was busy changing them through intercession. It seemed she was always there with her gentle reminder, "Roger, I'm praying for you."

One Sunday we visited another church to hear their guest speaker. Due to the crowd we had to take a pew near the back. As we settled into our seats, I felt a touch on my shoulder. I turned around and, there she *was*. "Roger, I'm praying for you."

Just as with our children, when we are born into God's family, we need to be trained in His ways. Not merely taught—*trained*.[313] We must learn not only to recognize His voice,[314] but to obey.[315]

There are going to be times when we will make mistakes.

> If we say that we have no sin, we deceive ourselves, and the truth is not in us.
>
> 1 John 1:8

But God has taken that into account and made provision to cover it.

> If we confess our sins,[316] He is faithful and just to forgive us our sins, and to cleanse us from all unrighteousness.
>
> 1 John 1:9

> "My little children," writes Paul, "these things write I unto you, that you sin not. And[317] if any man sin, we have an advocate with the Father, Jesus Christ the righteous. And He is the propitiation[318] for our sins. And not for ours only, but also for the sins of the whole world."
>
> 1 John 2:1–2

He is faithful to cleanse us *if*—if we will admit to our mistakes instead of trying to justify them or blame someone else as did Adam and Eve.[319]

Adam may have been the first to dream up the idea that the best defense is a good offence. At any rate, he got in God's face and accused *Him* for giving him a defective woman. That put Eve on the spot, so she turned and pointed to the serpent. During my lifetime I have tried that approach a number of times. But, like Adam, it has never worked for me either.

If you're anything like I am now, you don't like soiled britches *or* a polluted spirit. Well, there's good news. God is in the cleaning business. As we would take an article of clothing to our local cleaner to have a stain removed, so we can take a sin-stained heart to God and He will cleanse it. If that's a desire of your heart, pray now with the Psalmist:

> "Search me, O God, and know my heart. Try me, and know my thoughts. And see if there be any wicked way in me, and lead me in the way everlasting."
>
> Psalm 139:23–24

> "Wash me thoroughly from my iniquity, and cleanse me from my sin."
>
> Psalm 51:2

If you're still dragging around in your smelly old rags of self-righteousness, you may keep them if you like, but you don't have to.

> "Come now, and let us reason together," says the Lord. "Though your sins be as scarlet, they shall be as white as snow; though they be red like crimson, they shall be as wool."
>
> Isaiah 1:18

God has a fresh new robe, tailored just for you. That is, if you want it. Those who accept can celebrate with Isaiah:

> "I will greatly rejoice in the Lord. My soul shall be joyful in my God, for He has clothed me with the garments of salvation. He has covered me with the robe of righteousness, as a bridegroom decks himself with ornaments, and as a bride adorns herself with her jewels."
>
> Isaiah 61:10

That's why Jesus Christ and Him only. No other in all of history has been able to do for you what He has done. Not only has He provided the way for us to receive God's righteousness,[320] but also to remove our guilt.[321]

> For if the blood of bulls and of goats, and the ashes of an heifer sprinkling the unclean, sanctifies to the purifying of the flesh, how much more shall the blood of Christ, who through the eternal Spirit offered Himself without spot to God, purge your conscience from dead works to serve the living God?
>
> Hebrews 9:13–14

He is worthy of your affection, my friend. Are you worthy of His? By the way, I'm still my parents' son. Although there are those who teach it, God does not discard us just because we make a mistake,[322] even when as unpleasant as was my situation. Jesus has promised that,

> "All that the Father gives Me shall come to Me. And him that comes to Me I will in no wise cast out."
>
> John 6:37

The Power of Choice

When you were born into this world you had no say in the matter. You were not allowed to choose your family—mother or father. You were not asked in which country you would like to live or whether you wanted to be a boy or a girl. You were not consulted about your choice of hair color, how tall you would like to be or the size of your nose. Neither were you allowed to vote on which ethnic group you preferred. All those were decided for you by pre-existing, controlling factors.

But God took special note of you even as you were developing in the womb. King David wrote,

> "My substance was not hid from You, when I was made[323] in secret, and curiously wrought[324] in the lowest parts of the earth. Your eyes did see my substance, yet being unperfect,[325] and in Your book all my members were written, which in continuance were fashioned,[326] when as yet there was none of them."
>
> Psalm 139:15–16

You were not an accident nor an afterthought. God formed you in the womb because it brought Him great joy to bring you into the world.

> You are worthy, O Lord, to receive glory and honor and power. For You have created all things, and for Your pleasure they are and were created.
>
> Revelation 4:11

Of the world's billions of people, you are one of a kind. You may be critical of something about your appearance but, unlike us, God does not judge according to what we look like on the outside.

> But the Lord said unto Samuel, "Look not on his countenance, or on the height of his stature; because I have refused him. For the Lord sees not as man sees. For man looks on the outward appearance, but the Lord looks on the heart."
>
> 1 Samuel 16:7

You are unique, my friend. You are special. No other since the beginning of time has had your exceptional features, characteristics, or abilities. The difficulty arises when we deny that truth to others as well. If God does not judge us by the way we look, what would give us the right to judge others by the way they look? Even as grand as we may think ourselves to be, we do not have that authority.

As a teen, my best friend had straight, black hair. Many times I would have to wait for Joe as he stood before the mirror, arranging every strand just so. But as soon as he moved, a hair would fall out of place and back to the mirror he would go for more grooming. Now, I'm a different container. My hair was not as fine and had a tendency to curl just a little. And while I envied my friend for *his* hair, he was wishing he had hair just like mine.

We become discontented when we compare ourselves to others. Much of our inner peace lies in acknowledging the fact that we each are unlike any other. If we can be at peace with who we are, then we can accept others for who they are. If in our spirit we are restless and discontent, we will tend to find fault with others.

Many people turn to some form of cosmetic "fix," looking for an external solution to an internal problem. Let me assure you my friend, your hair is just the right color. Or if you have no hair, that's okay too. If your legs are long enough to reach the ground you're just the right height, and your nose fits your face nicely.

Every day we are bombarded with hundreds of messages designed to create discontent and to stir our desire for something different—or more—or "better." Millions are drowning in a sea of debt, brought about by their craving for "things." They spend money they can't afford or don't have, and then blame God for their lack. But God is not our problem.

A little cartoon opossum named Pogo once made the observation, "We have met the enemy, and he is us." That's good preaching, my friend. That is Biblical truth.

Acceptance of one's self is a matter of choice. Acceptance of others is also a choice. And this isn't limited to persons of a different color, nationality or beliefs. It includes husbands and wives–parents and children. The key lies, not in approval, but acceptance. Approval is based upon one's conduct in relation to our individual principles— acceptance or rejection must be based upon God's. Acceptance of the person does not obligate us to approve of their behavior, only to treat them as someone God has created and therefore values.

We must think as God thinks, not wishing for anyone to perish.[327] God instructed Ezekiel,

> "Say unto them, 'As I live,' says the Lord God, 'I have no pleasure in the death of the wicked; but that the wicked turn from his way and live. Turn you, turn you from your evil ways. For why will you die, O house of Israel?'"
>
> Ezekiel 33:11

The choice is yours and yours alone. Choose to accept yourself—choose to accept others—choose life. The authority is in your hands.

That Little Red Thing at the Bottom of the Pool

I was about fifteen years old—Kay was fourteen or so. We lived at the Cherry Point Marine Air Station in North Carolina. Swimming was one of my greatest passions. Kay was another. One day at the base swimming pool we were the only ones there with the exception of the Marine lifeguard. While I swam, Kay visited with the Marine. Jealous for her attention, I contrived a scheme by which to impress her.

The material of the time for men's swim suits was remarkably flexible. A small pair could easily expand to accommodate a somewhat larger individual. I had such a suit.

The water was clear and still. Climbing the seventeen-foot tower I walked to its edge. Breathing deeply as if trying to catch my breath, I watched Kay from the corner of my eye. The moment she looked my way I dove, executing a perfect one-and-one-half summersault.

The water parted with hardly a splash. Pleased with my grandstand dive I broke to the surface, knowing she had to have been impressed. But something didn't feel just right and, looking down, there, twelve feet below on the bottom of the pool lay my little red bathing suit. The angle of entry and force of the dive had peeled it right off my little show-off body.

No matter how hard we try to impress, the Bible warns that one day we will discover our "bathing trunks" lying on the bottom of the pool. All things are naked before the Lord.[328] As I learned the day of my grand dive, "Pride goes before destruction, and an haughty spirit before a fall."[329]

If we will not judge ourselves, God will do it for us.[330] If we refuse to humble ourselves, *He* will humble us, just as Moses said to the Israelites.

> "And you shall remember all the way which the Lord your God led you these forty years in the wilderness, to humble you, and to prove[331] you, to know what was in your heart, whether you would keep His commandments, or no.

> "And He humbled you, and suffered[332] you to hunger, and fed you with manna, which you knew not, neither did your fathers know; that He might make you know that man does not live by bread only, but by every word that proceeds out of the mouth of the Lord does man live."

Deuteronomy 8:2–3

What's New?

If you are a Christian, my friend, *you* are new. Paul tells us in 2 Corinthians 5:17, that if any man [one] is in Christ, he is a new creature. Old things are passed away and all things are new.

The concept of "new creature" is that of a brand new, never before existing, freshly created being. It carries the idea of a different nature from what is contrasted as old.[333] So, what's *new?* Well, for beginners, when we are born again we are cleansed from our sins[334] as though they never happened.[335] We have a better outlook on life.[336] We have the ability to do right.[337] God removes our rags of self-righteousness and clothes us in His robe of righteousness.[338] We are translated into his kingdom[339] where, positionally, we are seated with Christ beside God Himself.

> And every priest stands daily ministering and offering oftentimes the same sacrifices, which can never take away sins. But this man, after He had offered one sacrifice for sins for ever, sat down on the right hand of God.
>
> Hebrews 10:11–12

> But God, who is rich in mercy, for His great love wherewith He loved us, even when we were dead in sins, has quickened us together with Christ, (by grace you are saved,) and has raised us up together, and made us sit together in heavenly places in Christ Jesus.
>
> Ephesians 2:4–6

We're the same old clay jar, my friend, but our contents are different. We are impregnated with God's Spirit, the spirit of holiness.[340] No longer are we to lend our mouths to profanity and lying. We are to guard our eyes from lusting[341] and our hearts from evil thoughts.[342]

We are not without imperfections, but we're on our way.

> "Beloved," wrote John, "now are we the sons of God, and it does not yet appear what we shall be: but we know that, when He shall appear, we shall be like Him, for we shall see Him as He is."
>
> 1 John 3:2

The bad news is that, although the war is won, we still will face onslaught from the enemy. The good news is that we're not alone. Paul assures the Christian that,

> "...He which has begun a good work in you will perform it until the day of Jesus Christ."
>
> Philippians 1:6

and John tells us,

> "You are of God, little children, and have overcome them[343]: because greater is He that is in you, than he that is in the world."
>
> 1 John 4:4

> "For whatsoever is born of God overcomes the world: and this is the victory that overcomes the world, our faith."
>
> 1 John 5:4

Although God is at work to change us,[344] we also have a job to do.

> And every man that has this hope in Him purifies himself, even as He is pure.
>
> 1 John 3:2–3

Oh, my friend, Christianity is much more than a religion. It's a brand new race. Peter announces to the Christian,

"But you are a chosen generation, a royal priesthood, an holy nation, a peculiar[345] people; that you should show forth the praises of Him who has called you out of darkness into His marvelous light. Which in time past were not a people, but are now the people of God. Which had not obtained mercy, but now have obtained mercy."

1 Peter 2:9–10

The word used here for nation is *ethnos,* meaning a race, a tribe, a people. As Abraham's descendants evolved into a new race of people, so the Christian is a member of an entirely new and unique race of people. When one is born from above, he is born into a new people group—the family of God.

"For this cause," writes Paul, "I bow my knees unto the Father of our Lord Jesus Christ, of whom the whole family in heaven and earth is named."

Ephesians 3:14–15

Once a friend and I were discussing the Bible when I made a statement with which he did not agree. "*Next* thing you're going to tell me," he said, "is that Abraham wasn't a Jew."

"He *wasn't,*" I said. "There *were* no Jews yet."

"Oh, *Bob,*" he laughed, and walked away.

In the beginning there was no Jewish race. Abraham was of a different people.

And you shall speak and say before the Lord your God, "A Syrian[346] ready to perish was my father, and he went down into Egypt, and sojourned there with a few, and became there a nation, great, mighty, and populous."

Deuteronomy 26:5

God took one man, a man who would believe, and made of him a mighty nation which would become a *type* of the Christian nation. It was Abraham to whom He promised,

"...I will make of you a great nation, and I will bless you, and make your name great, and you shall be a blessing."

Genesis 12:2

Tossed Salad

We look for the Jew in the descendants of Abraham, Isaac and Jacob. But not all accepted into the nation of Israel were of natural lineage. Most notable is the Gentile blood that flowed through Ephraim and Manassah, two of the twelve tribes of Israel.[347] Although their father, Joseph, was a son of Israel, their mother, Asenath,[348] was an Egyptian, the daughter of Potipherah,[349] a priest of On.[350] There were also Egyptians who left with the Israelites in the exodus.[351]

Nor were all of God's "chosen" perfect. Matthew's genealogy of Joseph, husband of Mary, records Thamar, a Canaanitish woman who committed incest with her father in law[352]—Rahab, a prostitute of Jerico,[353]—Bathsheba, an adulteress,[354] and Ruth,[355] citizen of Moab, a nation rejected by God.[356]

There were also murderers, among whom were Simeon and Levi,[357] David,[358] and Paul, the great apostle.[359]

All throughout scripture we find evidence that God truly is no respecter of persons. And, as the Jewish leaders of Jesus' day, it angers us when God elevates those we deem to be of lesser value to our level.

> And He (Jesus) said, "Verily I say unto you, No prophet is accepted in his own country. But I tell you of a truth, many widows were in Israel in the days of Elijah, when the heaven was shut up three years and six months, when great famine was throughout all the

land but unto none of them was Elijah sent, save unto Sarepta, a
city of Sidon, unto a woman that was a widow.

"And many lepers were in Israel in the time of Elisha the prophet;
and none of them was cleansed, saving Naaman the Syrian."

And all they in the synagogue, when they heard these things, were
filled with wrath, and rose up, and thrust Him out of the city, and
led Him unto the brow of the hill whereon their city was built,
that they might cast Him down headlong.

Luke 4:24–29

Both the widow and Naaman were Gentiles, and it enraged the
Jews to be reminded that God had showed them a kindness over His
"chosen." But that's the family of God, my friend. Just a bunch of
fruit and vegetables picked from all the trees and gardens of life. It's
easy for us to condemn those religious folk who wanted to kill Jesus
because He exposed their bigotry. But what about us? Are we in that
bunch, or God's bunch? We may not go so far as to kill someone
physically, but do we wound emotionally with our words or attitude?
As God warned Simon Peter, neither must we call *any* man common
or unclean.[360]

"Them" and Us

It's natural for us to be drawn toward those we consider to be like ourselves. Therefore, the adage, "Birds of a feather, flock together," is a fitting description of man. But this tends to foster an attitude of exclusiveness. By its very definition, exclusive means to keep others out. Even Jesus' disciples thought themselves to be a pretty elite bunch.

Consider the incident of a certain woman of Canaan.[361]

> And then from there Jesus arose, and departed into the borders of Tyre and Sidon, and entered into a house, and would have no man know it, but He could not be hid. For, behold, a certain woman of Caanan came out of the same coasts, whose young daughter had an unclean spirit, heard of Him, and came and fell at His feet, and cried unto Him saying, "Have mercy on me, O Lord, son of David. My daughter is grievously vexed with a devil." The woman was Greek, a Syrophenician by nation, and she besought Him that He would cast forth the devil (demon) out of her daughter.
>
> But He answered her not a word. And His disciples came and besought Him, saying, "Send her away; for she cries after us."
>
> But He answered and said, "I am not sent but unto the lost sheep of the house of Israel."
>
> Then came she and worshipped Him, saying, "Lord, help me."

But Jesus answered and said unto her, "Let the children first be filled, for it is not meet to take the children's bread, and cast it unto the dogs."

And she answered and said unto Him, "Yes, truth, Lord. Yet the dogs under the table eat of the children's crumbs which fall from their master's table."

Then Jesus answered and He said unto her, "O woman, great is your faith. For this saying go your way. Be it unto you even as you will. The devil is gone out of your daughter."

And her daughter was made whole from that very hour. And when she was come to her house, she found the devil gone out, and her daughter laid upon the bed.

When reading a Scripture one thing is absolutely essential—it must always agree with all other scripture—and the word all, means *all,* not just some. So let's take a closer look at this account.

First, it is important to note that Jesus' reply, "I am not sent *but...,*" was not to the woman but the disciples.[362] Jesus was telling them that the Jew was not His only concern. At His dedication, a man named Simeon had said,

"Lord, now let Your servant depart[363] in peace, according to Your word. For my eyes have seen Your Salvation, which You have prepared before the face of all people.[364] A light to lighten the Gentiles, and the glory of Your people Israel."

Luke 2:25–32

Next, the word "dogs"[365] spoken to the woman is the Greek word, *kunarion,* meaning, a young puppy. Specifically, a little house puppy—a pet.

And so Jesus' response was not a rebuke as some teach, but a play on words, which the woman was quick to understand. Therefore, rather than taking offense, she replied, "That's true, Sir. But the little puppies eat the crumbs that fall from the master's table."

The Greek word for "but" in "I am not sent but unto the lost sheep of the house of Israel," is the word, *ei me,* and may be translated many ways: but, except (that), if not, more than, save (only) that, saving, till, just, etc.[366]

If we read, "I am not sent for any *except* for the lost sheep of the house of Israel," we make God to be a respecter of persons, and that is not consistent with other scripture. We note then that Jesus said, "I am *not* sent *but*—unto the lost sheep of the house of Israel." A more accurate understanding would be, "I am not sent *just* unto the lost sheep of the house of Israel." This interpretation is completely compatible with all other scripture.

We must always ask of any scripture, of all the accounts God could have had written into His one small book, why *this* one? What is the lesson He would have us learn, remembering that in order to disclose truth, it must be consistent with *all* other scripture.

Jesus said in John 10:16,

> "And other sheep I have, which are not of this fold. Them also I must bring, and they shall hear My voice; and there shall be one fold, and one shepherd."

So, who were those other sheep—those of whom the disciples were not aware? From beginning to end the Bible clearly evidences that the Gentiles[367] were always included in God's economy.[368] No one was left out—ever.

> And John answered Him, saying, "Master, we saw one casting out devils in Your name, and he follows not us. And we forbade him, because he follows not us."
>
> But Jesus said, "Forbid him not. For there is no man which shall do a miracle in My name, that can lightly speak evil of Me. For he that is not against us is on our part."
>
> Mark 9:38–40

Time and again Jesus' disciples would argue among themselves who would be the greatest in His kingdom.[369] Time and again He would have to remind them that God's kingdom was made up of servants, not masters—children, not fathers—the humble, not big shots.

Dennis the Menace said it best when he told his little friend, "The secret, Joey, is to know you're somebody, without thinking you're somebody."[370]

No Afro-Christians

Not long after accepting Christ I bought my first new Bible. On its cover I had imprinted, "Roger L. Roberson, Jr., Evangelist." One day a pastor noticed and cautioned me about labels. The lettering has long since worn away but I have never forgotten his advice.

Labels are essential in identification but can be destructive if misused. This is especially true of people. We have a tendency to live out, and even capitalize on our label. If we are convinced our label is accurate, we will become that which we have been classified.

If we grow up with criticism we feel we are insignificant and will never rise to our potential until we change our label. On the other hand, labels that affirm inspire us to great accomplishments. Therefore, what one believes of him or her self is crucial.[371]

It is natural for one to be drawn toward those of his own kind. But issues arise when groups or individuals set themselves apart from those that are different. And that's what the Hyphen does. As a people we have categorized, divided, sub-divided, classified, grouped, pigeonholed, typed and sorted until our Nation, as with all previous nations, is becoming unraveled. Though still stamped on our coins, E Pluribus Unum[372] is fading from our hearts and we are fast becoming a nation of E Unum Pluribus.[373]

Instead of Americans we now are Afro-Americans, Native-Americans, Irish-Americans, Italian-Americans,...And instead of Christians, we are Protestant-Christians, Catholic-Christians, Presbyterian-Christians, and many, many others. This is not the work of God, my friend, but the enemy.

God has spoken plainly. In His kingdom there are no Afro-Christians, Caucasian-Christians, Irish-Christians, or Italian-Christians. There are only Christians.[374]

> "Neither pray I for these alone," said Jesus, "but for them also which shall believe on Me through their word; that they all may be one; as You, Father, are in Me, and I in You, that they also may be one in us: that the world may believe that You have sent Me."
>
> John 17:20–21

One, my friend. One! If you are a Christian you are one with all other Christians, and your nature is to desire the best for *all* people. *No* one who harbors hate or disrespect for another is a Christian, regardless of what they might profess.

Black skin does not earn one free access into heaven. But all Christians who are black will be received with great joy. Nor does white skin receive preferential treatment. Neither whiteness nor blackness will earn special favor from God. He is not moved by the color of our skin, only the color of our heart.[375] But all Christ-like ones, whether black, white, red, yellow, or brown—*all* will join their brothers and sisters around the throne of their Creator Father.

Follow the Leader

The cross was not for the innocent but the guilty. The cross was meant for me—it was meant for you. *But God…*

> …has made Him (Jesus) to be sin for us, Who knew no sin, that we might be made the righteousness of God in Him.
>
> 2 Corinthians 5:21

It does not please God for anyone to perish,[376] not even the wicked.[377] That's why He sent Jesus to take our place on the cross. No one took Jesus' life. He and His Father *gave*.[378]

Hundreds of years before Jesus' incarnation Isaiah prophesied of His faithfulness to the will of His Father.

> "The Lord God has opened My ear, and I was not rebellious, neither turned away back. I gave My back to the smiters, and My cheeks to them that plucked off the hair.[379] I hid not My face from shame and spitting[380] for the Lord God will help Me. Therefore shall I not be confounded.[381] Therefore have I set My face like a flint,[382] and I know that I shall not be ashamed."[383]
>
> Isaiah 50:5–7[384]

"I *gave*…" None of what Jesus endured was an afterthought.[385] It was in God's plans even before He created the world and man.

> Forasmuch as you know that you were not redeemed with corruptible things, as silver and gold, from your vain[386] conversa-

tion[387] received by tradition from your fathers, but with the precious blood of Christ, as of a lamb without blemish and without spot. Who verily was foreordained[388] *before the foundation of the world*, but was manifest[389] in these last times for you.

1 Peter 1:18–20

And all that dwell upon the earth shall worship Him, whose names are not written in the book of life of the Lamb slain *from the foundation[390] of the world.*

Revelation 13:8

During World War II at a Japanese concentration camp, a detail of prisoners returned to the compound after having completed a work assignment. When the tools were counted, one shovel was thought to be missing. When no one admitted to having taken it, the officer in charge of the detail warned that if the offender did not confess, a prisoner would be shot every ten minutes until the shovel was returned.

After a few moments of silence, one of the prisoners stepped forward and was instantly shot. A subsequent inventory revealed all tools accounted for. The shovel had not been missing after all.

According to Jesus, that prisoner loved. He made the ultimate sacrifice to save the lives of his friends. And so it was with Jesus.[391]

> For Christ also has once suffered for sins, the just for the unjust, that He might bring us to God, being put to death in the flesh, but quickened by the Spirit.
>
> 1 Peter 3:18

He did not have to submit to the humiliation, the suffering and death.[392] In truth, Jesus did not want to endure the pain and suffering He knew was to come.

> And He went a little further, and fell on His face, and prayed, saying, "O my Father, if it be possible, let this cup pass from Me. Nevertheless not as I will, but as You will." And He left them, and went away again, and prayed the third time, saying the same words.
>
> Matthew 26:39, 44

But because God loves you, Jesus humbled Himself and submitted to His Father's plan of redemption, taking upon Himself the punishment for your offences.

> "Now is My soul troubled," He prayed. "And what shall I say, 'Father, save Me from this hour?' But for this cause came I unto this hour."
>
> John 12:27

Throughout His trial Jesus faced His accusers in silence.

> He was oppressed, and He was afflicted, yet He opened not His mouth. He is brought as a lamb to the slaughter, and as a sheep before her shearers is dumb, so He opened not His mouth.[393]
>
> Isaiah 53:7

> And the chief priests accused Him of many things, but He answered nothing. And Pilate asked Him again, saying, "Answer You nothing? Behold how many things they witness against You." But Jesus yet answered nothing, so that Pilate marveled.
>
> Mark 15:3–5

Jesus refused to defend Himself because He was identifying with us. And since we all are guilty, He had no defense. Christ loves us so much, that He put our welfare above His own comfort, setting the example we are to follow.

> "You call Me Master and Lord," He said, "and you say well, for so I am. If I then, your Lord and Master, have washed your feet,[394] you also ought to wash one another's feet. For I have given you an example, that you should do as I have done to you."
>
> John 13:13–15

Therefore,

> Let nothing be done through strife or vainglory,[395] but in lowliness of mind[396] let each esteem other better than themselves. Look not every man on his own things, but every man also on the things of others. Let this mind be in you, which was also in Christ Jesus.
>
> Philippians 2:3–5

Battle for the Soul

Horrified by the atrocities some commit upon others, especially where little children are concerned, we question how anyone could do such things to another human. But we're not excused. Although the degree of our offence may seem trivial by comparison, we too are offenders in need of forgiveness.

> "Whosoever shall keep the whole law," writes James, "and yet offend in one point, he is guilty of all."
>
> James 2:10

We may protest that we are not prejudiced. We may profess to love others. But how much love have we for someone if we drag them into the darkened chambers of our heart[397] and there lust after them?—or rape?—or degrade?—or slander?—or criticize?—or ridicule?

Consequently, we have no defense for thinking ourselves better than someone else. Even a small sin nullifies our righteousness.

> Your glorying is not good. Don't you know that a little leaven leavens the whole lump?
>
> 1 Corinthians 5:6

We are in a war, my friend. Lucifer[398] rebelled against God and was stripped of his position and glory.[399] Seeking vengeance, he turned to attack God's creation.[400] His strategy is to lure us into sin by appealing to our desires.

> Every man is tempted, when he is drawn away of his own lust, and enticed.[401] Then when lust has conceived, it brings forth sin. And sin, when it is finished, brings forth death.
>
> James 1:14–15

We may declare our love for God and that we would never have anything to do with Satan. But we must not allow ourselves to be lulled into a false sense of security. At no time are we immune from his attacks.[402]

As it was with Paul, we too are in a relentless battle with our passions and our pride.

> "I see another law in my members, warring against the law of my mind," he wrote, "and bringing me into captivity to the law of sin, which is in my members."
>
> Romans 7:23

> "For the flesh lusts against the Spirit, and the Spirit against the flesh, and these are contrary the one to the other so that you cannot do the things that you would."
>
> Galatians 5:17

Even Christ's most faithful swore they would never stumble.

> "Though all men shall be offended because of You," protested Peter, "yet will I never be offended. Though I should die with You, yet will I not deny You." Likewise also said all the disciples.
>
> Matthew 26:33, 35

At some point in our lives, we all have regretted doing something we should not have done, or neglected to do something we knew we should. We want to do what is right, but often fall short. The problem is, being descended from Adam, we have inherited his characteristics. We are not sinners because we sin, we sin because we are sinners, remember? It is in our nature to sin. It is reality we must fully realize. Consequently, powerless to live free from sin's attacks, we agonize with the apostle Paul,

> "That which I do I allow not.[403] For what I would, that do I not, but what I hate, that do I."
>
> Romans 7:15

We are in a life and death struggle, and although we often tire, the enemy never does.

> For we wrestle not against flesh and blood, but against principalities, against powers, against the rulers of the darkness of this world, against spiritual wickedness in high places.
>
> Ephesians 6:12

As with Simon Peter, Christ warns us as well.

> "...Behold, Satan has desired to have you, that he may sift you as wheat. But I have prayed for you," He said, "that your faith fail not."[404]
>
> Luke 22:31–32a

At times it may seem that we have been singled out for Satan's attacks. Beaten and discouraged by life's challenges, we may feel all hope gone. If that's you, take heart. Don't give up. God is on our side and His Son is praying for you[405]—white man, black man, red man, brown man, yellow man—*all* men. He believes in you, my friend. He is for you.

God Is With You, Mighty Warrior

Doug Harrison, August 7, 2003[406]

A battle rages in me, a battle for my soul,
On one side stands a Holy God, the other His vile foe.
I lay upon the battlefield, my body bruised and torn,
The weapons I use for my defense lay scattered, broken and worn.

I hear the bugles of retreat; the enemy's advance draws near,
My allies have abandoned me; my heart is filled with fear.
I hear the roar of Satan; I hear the cries of pain,
The battlefield is covered with those that he has slain.

With fear and apprehension, I turn to face my foe,
I raise my damaged shield of faith to face life's ending blow.
Then suddenly a battle cry, a sound of victory,
I watch the army of my foe, retreat, and then they flee.

For charging onto the battlefield, with sword and shield held high,
Is the Captain of my army, the savior of my life.
With strength renewed and hope restored, His army presses on,
My Captain lifts me to my feet, to urge me further on.

While the battle rages round me, I hear my Captain say,
"God is with you mighty warrior, live to fight another day!"

But as much as God loves us, it isn't just about us. As God would do for us, we are to do for others.

> "Brethren," writes Paul, "if a man be overtaken in a fault, you which are spiritual, restore such an one in the spirit of meekness; considering yourself, lest you also be tempted. Bear one another's burdens, and so fulfil the law of Christ. For if a man think himself to be something, when he is nothing, he deceives himself."
>
> Galatians 6:1–3

> "And let us not be weary in well doing: for in due season we shall reap, if we faint not. As we have therefore opportunity, let us do good unto all men, especially unto them who are of the household of faith."
>
> Galatians 6:7–10

THE GIFT

Most of us would agree that we should love others. But it isn't always easy. Even if we would like to we're not always able. That's because the principal issue is not about black and white, who's right or who's wrong. The principal issue is the heart—it's about our sin nature.

More importantly it's about where we will spend eternity. If *Heaven* is real then Hell must be also, for Jesus spoke more of Hell than of Heaven. Not as a threat but a warning, so that we might avoid it. Hell was never intended as punishment for mankind.[407] The cross is proof of God's love, and the extent to which He was willing to go to save us from it.

But God will not save one who refuses to be saved. That would be coercion. God is love,[408] and love cannot be demanded, it must be given willingly. Therefore the choice is ours and ours only. But God *pleads* with us to choose life.

> "I call[409] heaven and earth to record[410] this day against you, that I have set before you life and death, blessing and cursing. Therefore choose life, that both you and your seed[411] may live."
>
> Deuteronomy 30:19–20

Jesus was willing to endure the pain, the humiliation and the rejection because He understands the dreadful despair of being separated from God.

And at the ninth hour Jesus cried with a loud voice, saying, "Eloi,

Eloi, lama sabachthani?" Which is, being interpreted, "My God, My God, why have You forsaken Me?"

Mark 15:34

He knows the horrors of an eternal, unforgiving Hell and does not want us to spend eternity there. Rejection of eternal life is acceptance of eternal damnation, and it causes Him to weep for us,[412] just as He wept over Jerusalem,

"O Jerusalem, Jerusalem! You that kill[413] the prophets, and stone them which are sent unto you, how often would I have gathered your children together, even as a hen gathers her chickens under her wings, and[414] you would not [let Me]!"

Matthew 23:37

While in the Navy, as our ship was docked at San Diego, California, a shipmate returned from liberty one day with cuts and scratches over most of his body. While swimming at La Jolla beach, he had heard a cry for help and looked to see a man struggling in the surf. My friend swam for the man and pulled him to safety. In the process, he had been pounded against the rocks and coral that lined the shore.

When the man was safely on the beach, he simply turned and walked away with not even a "Thank you." My friend said he was so angry he felt like throwing the guy back into the surf.

But God and His Christ have done much more than that for us. And just as the man saved from the crashing waves of La Jolla, many have turned and, without a word of gratitude, walked away from their Savior.

How about you? Are you thankful for what He suffered so that you might escape eternal destruction and receive eternal life? Do you tell Him? Or have you too just walked away? If you were to die tonight—this minute—do you know that you would go to be with the Father in Heaven?

For God so loved, my friend, that He *gave*, that we might have eternal[415] and abundant life.[416] Have you received? If not, settle it now. Only through the One who *is* love, can we truly love others.

Finally, brethren, whatsoever things are true, whatsoever things are honest, whatsoever things are just, whatsoever things are pure, whatsoever things are lovely, whatsoever things are of good report, if there be any virtue, and if there be any praise, think on these things.

Philippians 4:8

Let no corrupt[417] communication[418] proceed out of your mouth, but that which is good to the use of edifying,[419] that it may minister grace unto the hearers.

And grieve[420] not the Holy Spirit of God, whereby you are sealed unto the day of redemption. Let all bitterness, and wrath,[421] and anger, and clamor,[422] and evil speaking,[423] be put away from you, with all malice,[424] and be kind one to another, tenderhearted,[425] forgiving one another, even as God for Christ's sake has forgiven you.

Ephesians 4:29–32

Eternal life hangs upon only two issues—loving God, and loving others.[426] And therein lies our life's struggle. At the end of his life Paul was able to say with confidence,

"I have fought a good fight, I have finished my course, I have kept the faith."

2 Timothy 4:7

May that be our epitaph as well, yours and mine, when it comes our time to cross into God's Heaven. Having freely received the gift of God's love,[427] let us in turn, freely give to all men—*all* men.

Amen

Salvation is Good News

The 4 Spiritual Laws

God loves you.

Sin separates you from God.

Jesus died for your sins.

You can be saved by confessing Jesus is Lord.

> The word is near you, even in your mouth, and in your heart. That is, the word of faith, which we preach. That if you shall confess with your mouth the Lord Jesus, and shall believe in your heart that God has raised Him from the dead, you shall be saved. For with the heart man believes unto righteousness, and with the mouth confession is made unto salvation.
>
> Romans 10:8–10

If you have never surrendered your life to God, pray this prayer.

"Heavenly Father, I believe You love me. I believe Jesus died for me and rose from the dead. Today, I confess Jesus as my Lord and receive the forgiveness of all my sins. Holy Spirit, come into my life. Thank You for saving me, in Jesus' name.

–Amen"

TYPOLOGY

From the very beginning, God set into His creation those things that would reflect Himself and His kingdom. He is revealed throughout all His creation, including mankind. Everything God created was made to point to Himself—to reveal His loves, His desires, His goals, His emotions, His nature. This is known as Typology.

Typology is:

1   A doctrine (teaching) based on types.

2   The study of, or analysis, or classification based on types.

Type means: 1- impression, model; 2- A person or thing (as in the Old Testament) believed to foreshadow another (as in the New Testament); 3- One having qualities of a higher value. (Webster's Dictionary).

Types are shadows of things to come.

Typology is peculiar to the Bible.

Types are never perfect.

Types must always go from the natural to the spiritual.

The created must always typify the Creator.

Our interpretation of types and symbols must be in harmony with the continuity of all scripture.

"No other book has, or could have, any of the kind of typology found in the Bible. It is the way God has chosen to record history before it happens. One is given in the natural and the other in the spiritual. Paul tells us in 1 Corinthians 15:46, 'There is the natural and *afterward* the spiritual.'

"God gave the history before it happened, in type, and then millenniums afterwards, when the antitype came, it was exactly as the type had revealed it." [Excerpted from the book, *Bible Typology*, by O.L. Johnson, page 2. Published by Harmony Press, Inc., Bourbon, Indiana 46504].[428]

God Revealed In Shadows, Patterns, Types and Images.

1   *Shadows:* Colossians 2:16–17, Hebrews 8:5, Hebrews 10:1

2   *Figures:* Romans 5:14, Hebrews 9:8–9, Hebrews 11:18–19, 1 Peter 3:20–21

3   *Patterns:* 1 Timothy 1:16, Hebrews 8:5, Hebrews 9:23,

4   *Examples:* Hebrews 8:5

5   *Image:* 2 Corinthians 4:4, Colossians 1:12–15, Hebrews 1:1–3, Hebrews 10:1

Examples of Type:

1   *Abraham and Isaac:* Genesis 22:1–13429

2   *Adam:* 1 Corinthians 15:45–49; Romans 5:14

3   *Christ, our Passover:* Compare 1 Corinthians 5:7–8 with Exodus 12:1–13, 21–23.

4   Circumcision: Romans 2:28–29

5   *Dove:* Luke 3:22

6   *Fiery* (brazen) Serpent: Numbers 21:8430

7   *Law:* Hebrews 10:1

8   *Man:* Genesis 1:26–27

9   *Manna:* Exodus 16:2–4; John 6:48–51

10 *Melchisedec:* Hebrews 5:5–6. Compare Genesis 14:18 with Luke 22:17–20

11 *Parables*

12 *Priest's Office:* Hebrews 8:4–5a

13 *Rituals:* Colossians 2:16–17

14 *The Rock* That Produced Water: Exodus 17:6; Numbers 20:11–12; 1 Corinthians 10:4

15 *The Scriptures, People, Tabernacle and Vessels of the Tabernacle:* Hebrews 9:19&21–23

BIBLIOGRAPHY

"Bible Typology," by O. L. Johnson, ©1963, 1976. Printed by Harmony Press, Inc., Bourbon, Indiana 46504

Jim Crow Legislation Overview, by Susan Falck, M.A., Research Associate, Cal State University, Northridge, Ca.

Newsweek Magazine, November 7, 2005, U.S. Edition.

Preamble to The Declaration of Independence

Samuel Morris, The Apostle of Simple Faith, Barbour Publishing, Uhrichsville, Ohio

Smith's Bible Dictionary, © 1948 by Zondervan Publishing House, Grand Rapids, Michigan, 49506

So What's The Difference? By Fritz Ridenour. ©1967, 1979, 2001 by Fritz Ridenour–ref. Moses 7:7,22 in *The Pearl of Great Price,* published by The Church of Jesus Christ of Latter Day Saints

The Holy Bible. King James Authorized Version.

The Living Word, King James Version, © 1964 by Joseph W. Cain Publisher, San Antonio, Texas,

The Tulsa World newspaper. World Publishing Company, Tulsa, Oklahoma

The Wall Street Journal, Review & Outlook, Englewood, Colorado

The World Book Encyclopedia © 2004 World Book, Inc., Chicago, Illinois

Vine's Expository Dictionary of Biblical Words, © 1984 by Thomas Nelson Publishers, Nashville, Tennessee

End Notes

1   Pastor of Victory Christian Center, Tulsa, OK. www.victory.com
2   Genesis 3:6
3   Genesis 2:17
4   Genesis 4:8
5   Hebrews 11:4; 1 John 3:12
6   Genesis 4:23
7   Genesis 25:29–34
8   Genesis 27:6–17
9   Genesis 37:3,4, 18–20; Acts 7:9
10   Statistic recorded in 2005
11   pastor of Victory Christian Center in Tulsa, Oklahoma.
12   "Knocked Down But Not Out," available at www.destinyimage.com or victory.com
13   See the account in Genesis 9:19–25
14   property, cattle, livestock.
15   Note that New York is not a *Southern* state
16   Source: *Jim Crow Legislation Overview,* by Susan Falck, M.A., Research Associate, Cal State University, Northridge, Ca.
17   As reported by http://www.blackgenocide.org/negro03.html:
18   The Birth Control Federation of America (original designation of Planned Parenthood)

"The Negro Project" - Margaret Sanger's Eugenic Plan for Black Americans.

my nickname

John 3:16

2 Peter 3:9

Romans 5:8

Hebrews chapters 8, 9 and 10

Genesis 1:27

Psalm 19:1

divinity

Matthew 22:37–40

©World Book, Inc.

sides

hayah

maowr

obscure, unclear; i.e., in a dim light

i.e., appears as a messenger of truth

farmer

naked

outside

did not look at

love

i.e., faults, shortcomings

expose

Genesis 4:8

ref. *So What's The Difference?* By Fritz Ridenour. ©1967, 1979, 2001 by Fritz Ridenour–ref. Moses 7:7,22 in *The Pearl of Great Price,* published by The Church of Jesus Christ of Latter Day Saints.

Moses

Isaiah 39:1

Isaiah 39:4

2 Kings 24:11–14

Reported in the Tulsa World, October 25, 2005.

As of 2005

Newsweek magazine, November 7, 2005, U.S. Edition.

Discipline; instruct.

Leviticus chapter 18

the Amorites were descendants of Caanan <Genesis 10:16> - The Old Testament frequently uses "Amorites" as a synonym for Canaanites in general.

Exodus 23:24

Song of Solomon 1:5

Acts 10:34, 35

Romans 3:23

1 John 4:8, 16

1 Samuel 16:7

Genesis 1:18, 9:1

mud, clay - Genesis 3:19

person

Greek *tselem:* (tseh'-lem); i.e. (figuratively) illusion, resemblance; hence, a representative figure, especially an idol. mankind is merely a "shadow" of God. Jesus Christ is the exact likeness. Hebrews 1:3 See also 1 Corinthians 15:44

person

whitewashed tombs

created/made

inward parts

concealed

created

body

created

i.e., out of view

fabricated, woven

womb

examined, (chose)

embryo

not yet fully formed

parts

described

the day

(to mold into a form, especially as a potter)

82   that is,. "when none of my parts existed," i.e., "when I did not exist."

83   i.e., "understand this"

84   clay, earth

85   Romans 5:14

86   Hebrews 11:4

87   Romans 3:23, 5:12

88   the same

89   Paul is speaking to the church. He is saying that Christ is in all Christians, not all men.

90   ref.: "Samuel Morris, The Apostle of Simple Faith"; Barbour Publishing

91   see The World Book Encyclopedia under African Americans

92   World Book Encyclopedia, 2005

93   leader of the Nation of Islam, a religious organization historically related to the Black Muslims - favors racial separation, black nationalism, and economic independence for African Americans. (2005 World Book Encyclopedia)

94   Review & Outlook, Wall Street Journal, June 30, 1994.

95   Matthew 24:6; Mark 13:7; Luke 21:9

96   Romans 8:22

97   quarreled, day after day

98   Romans 5:14

99   1 Timothy 2:14

100   Luke 13:31

101   John 3:1, John 19:37–40

102   Luke 7:1–5; Acts 10:1–2

103   Romans 2:11–15

104   Romans 3:23

105   Matthew 22:37–38; 1 John 20:21 a brotherhood. Vine's Expository Dictionary of Biblical Words

106   source: public domain

107   Luke 23:34a

108   the bright, shinning one

109   false accuser, slanderer

110 John 10:10
111 Romans 10:17
112 Proverbs 23:7
113 Genesis 3:1–6
114 Matthew 4:1–9
115 James 1:14; 1 John 2:16
116 2 Corinthians 11:14–15
117 Hebrews 11:25
118 Acts 19:13–17
     hostility
     Satan
121 plural, descendants, i. e., mankind
122 singular, one individual, i. e., Jesus
123 He, the seed
124 John 8:44
     fallen angels
126 John 6:70, John 8:41, 44
127 as of 2006
128 Mark 5:6–11
129 Acts 9:5, 26:14–Goad: a sharp point, to prick, sting.
     Romans 6:6
     Romans 5:8
132 Psalm 51:5
133 Jeremiah 17:9
134 Numbers 32:23
135 1 Peter 5:8
136 Exodus 3:13–14
137 princes
138 Matthew 26:47,55; Mark 14:43,49; Luke 22:52,53; John 18:3,12.
139 Strong's Exhaustive Concordance of the Bible, Hendrickson Publishers, Peabody, MA, 01961–3473
140 to be weak, sick, afflicted, diseased. Vine's Expository Dictionary of Biblical Words
141 Strong's Exhaustive Concordance
142 the Son

143   Exodus 9:16; John 6:70–71
144   ref. Psalm 2
145   appearance
146   disfigured
147   shape, body
148   Mark 15:9–10
149   Luke 23:4; John 19:4, 6
150   John 19:12 (sought = searched, inquired for a way)
151   to train up a child, teach, i.e. by implication, discipline (by
       punishment).
152   Acts 22:24–In the Old Testament, scourge is generally a
       word that describes punishment. In the New Testament,
       to be "examined under scourging" referred to an investiga-
       tion, which began with the beating of the prisoner. (Vine's
       Expository Dictionary of Biblical Words.)
153   John 1:29; Revelation 13:8
154   1 Peter 1:18–20
155   Genesis 3:15
156   uproar
157   compare with Deuteronomy 21:1–9
158   authority
159   i.e., "You are not in control."
160   Note: Here the word *he* is in italics, indicating it was not in
       the manuscripts, but added for clarification. Compare with
       Exodus 3:14
161   see also Luke 4:28–30
162   2 Timothy 3:1–5
163   personal
164   introduce secretly
165   dangerous choices
166   filthy, wantonness
167   greed
168   fabricated, made up
169   John 10:10a
170   John 3:17
171   Luke 19:10

172   1 John 3:8

173   Luke 5:32

174   John 10:10

175   Luke 4:18

176   1 Corinthians 6:20, 7:23

177   "Crimson River," by Robyn Gomez–from her CD, "Long-ing" www.robyngomez.com

178   Genesis 3:7–10; Isaiah 53:3

179   2 Corinthians 6:14–15

180   the menstrual flux (as periodical)

181   "removed us," i.e., from God's presence

182   do willfully, a continuous habit, i.e., practice

183   unmistakable

184   i.e., fellow man

185   John 8:31,32

186   2 Peter 3:9

187   did not want

188   truth

189   creation. a brand new, never before existing being

190   1 John 2:1

191   Romans 3:23, 5:12–"missed the mark."

192   gospel

193   Mark 2:17

194   a cursory review of the Scriptures reveals that saints are those who belong to Christ, not "special" persons who are canonized by a particular group or organization. Psalm 50:5 and others

195   admit

196   a "missing of the mark." Vine's Expository Dictionary.

197   the natural birth vs the spiritual birth

198   wishes

199   teacher

200   Ephesians 4:17–19

201   Ephesians 2:2–3

202   John 4:24

203   from above

204   Who. See John 1:1–4, 14; Revelation 19:11–13
205   John 3:5
206   i.e., understand John 3:3
207   ability and authority
208   children
209   Genesis, chapter 1
210   fill
211   wages
212   a wandering, a forsaking of the right path
213   necessary. See Leviticus 18:22 & 20:13
214   See *Typology.*
215   John 1:13
216   hot anger, passion
217   Matthew 13:18–23
218   Deuteronomy 22:23, 24
219   Luke 1:35
220   Colossians 2:9
221   i.e., die, "sown"
222   speaking of His death, burial and resurrection
223   the product of the creative act.
224   purchased; 1 Corinthians 6:20, 7:23
225   Matthew 13:18–23; Mark 4:13–20; Luke 8:11–15
226   1 Thessalonians 5:19
227   God's Word, Jesus
228   John 1:12–compare with John 6:66
229   as a husband cares for his wife, as a father cares for his children.
230   Matthew 11:28
231   Jesus, the Christ
232   John 1:12; 1 John 5:12
233   2 Corinthians 6:2
234   Matthew 6:9
235   Psalm 51:10
236   See *Typology* under Notes.
237   Colossians 1:27
238   Ezekiel 36:24–27

239	2 Corinthians 5:17
240	Galatians 5:22–23
241	Philippians 3:13–15
242	vomit
243	our fleshly desires
244	behavior, manner of life (of)
245	our old lifestyle
246	our new lifestyle
247	passions
248	a longing, especially for what is forbidden
249	self-conceit
250	to stir up what is evil in another, i.e. (by implicate, to irritate)
251	Thing that you long for
252	Romans 1:19,20
253	Isaiah 1:10–17
254	Isaiah 1:18; Revelation 3:20
255	Godlike
256	disposition, personality
257	Malachi 3:6
258	John 3:8
259	Luke 1:34
260	the Spirit of Holiness. See Romans 1:4
261	Leviticus 11:44, 45
262	John 4:24
263	John 1:1–3
264	Luke 1:31
265	divorce her
266	quietly
267	Divinity
268	in a body
269	the physical birth
270	the spiritual birth
271	i.e., Jesus
272	1 Peter 1:23
273	to glue, stick to
274	Matthew 1:23

275	existed
276	Him
277	existed
278	John 17:23–26
279	Ezekiel 28:12
280	Ezekiel 28:13
281	Ezekiel 28:13
282	Ezekiel 28:16
283	Isaiah 14:11; Ezekiel 28:15
284	Isaiah 14:13–14
285	splendor
286	Mark 3:23–26
287	Job 1:6, 2:1
288	messengers
289	to protect. See Genesis 3:24 and Exodus 25:17–22.
290	Proverbs 14:12, 16:25
291	Genesis 2:16–17
292	Genesis 2:23 (emphatically)
293	John 13:27
294	1 John 2:16
295	Genesis 3:6
296	Compare to 1 Timothy 2:11–15
297	John 12:49–50
298	complete
299	i.e., treats as inferior
300	Genesis 3:8–9
301	John 3:16
302	John 14:6
303	God and mankind
304	united
305	See also Matthew 26:62–63; John 19:10;
306	Isaiah 53:5
307	Romans 3:22–23
308	Hebrews 4:16
309	1 John 3:8
310	John 19:30

311 Psalm 110:10; Proverbs 9:10
312 Isaiah 51:1
313 Deuteronomy 6:5–7, 11:17–19
314 John 10:27
315 Luke 6:46
316 admit failings
317 but
318 atonement, appeasement
319 Genesis 3:11–13
320 2 Corinthians 5:21
321 Romans 8:1
322 Romans 8:35–39
323 created
324 to vary color, i.e. embroider; by implication, to fabricate. - needlework, curiously work.
325 a wrapped (and unformed mass, i.e. as the embryo).
326 (through the squeezing into shape); to mold into a form; especially as a potter.
327 2 Peter 3:9
328 Hebrews 4:13
329 Proverbs 16:18
330 Luke 6:37
331 test
332 allowed
333 Vine's Expository Dictionary.
334 Ezekiel 36:25; Isaiah 1:18; 1 Corinthians 6:9–11
335 Jeremiah 31:33–34
336 Ezekiel 36:26
337 Ezekiel 36:27
338 2 Corinthians 5:21–compare Exodus 28:15, 29, and 30 with Ephesians 6:14.
339 Colossians 1:13
340 Romans 1:4
341 Job 31:1
342 Philippians 4:8
343 evil spirits, thoughts, desires

344	Philippians 1:6
345	purchased, preserved
346	Aramite, or Aramaean
347	Genesis 41:50–52
348	peril, misfortune
349	that scatters abroad, or demolish. Priest in the worship of the sun
350	Heliopolis, "city of the sun."
351	Exodus 12:37–38
352	Matthew 1:3; Genesis 38:1–26
353	Matthew 1:5; Hebrews 11:31
354	Matthew 1:6; 2 Samuel 11:1–4. Possibly a Hittite, being wife of Uriah the Hittite
355	Ruth 1:1, 4
356	Matthew 1:3, 5–6
357	Genesis 34
358	2 Samuel 11:1–25
359	Acts 7:59, 22:20; Galatians 1:13
360	Acts 10:28
361	Matthew 15:21–28; Mark 7:24–30
362	Matthew 15:23–24
363	die
364	i.e., where everyone can see
365	Matthew 15:26; Mark 7:27
366	Strong's Exhaustive Concordance
367	any non-Jew
368	Genesis 12:3; Galatians 3:8
369	Matthew 18:1; Mark 9:34
370	North American Syndicate
371	Proverbs 23:6–7
372	"Out of many, one."
373	"Out of one, many."
374	Christ like ones
375	1 Samuel 16:7
376	2 Peter 3:9
377	Ezekiel 33:11

378   John 3:16
379   Matthew 26:67, 68
380   ridicule
381   to taunt, or insult
382   Luke 9:51
383   disappointed
384   compare with Luke 9:51–53
385   pictured in Genesis 22:1–13
386   empty, unprofitable
387   behavior, conduct
388   known beforehand
389   revealed
390   founding
391   John 15:13
392   Matthew 26:52–53
393   i.e., did not defend himself
394   i.e., served you
395   self conceit
396   humility
397   thoughts, mind
398   *haylel:* the morning star
399   Isaiah 14:12–14
400   I Peter 5:8
401   "lured by a bait"
402   I Peter 5:8
403   i.e., "I don't understand why I do what I do."
404   John 17:20–21
405   Luke 22:32a
406   Used by permission
407   Matthew 25:41
408   I John 4:8, 16
409   subpoena
410   witness
411   children
412   John 17:20–21
413   murder

but
John 3:16
John 10:10
rotten, i.e. worthless
something said
that which builds up
cause pain, sorrow
hot anger, passion
the tumult of controversy
vilification, (especially against God)
badness, wickedness, maliciousness
compassionate, i.e. sympathetic
Matthew 22:37–40
Matthew 10:7–8
Public domain. Used with permission
Picturing the death, burial and resurrection of Christ. Ref.
Hebrews 11:17–19
pictures Christ on the cross.